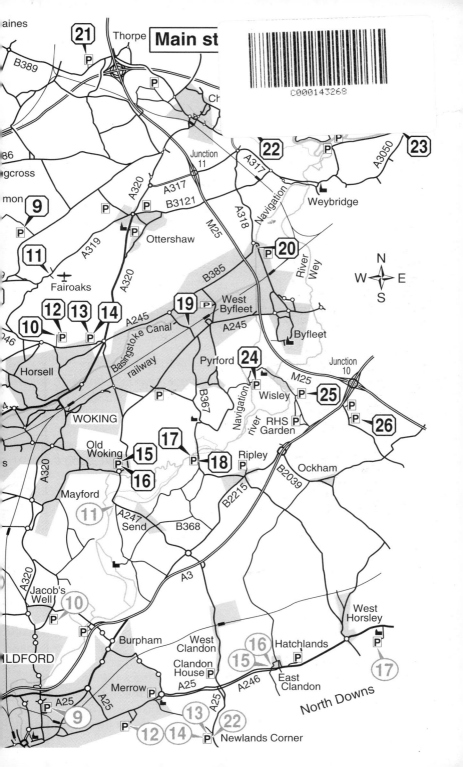

1 West End, Brentmoor and Brook Place

About 6½ km/4miles over heath and farmland with a 1½ km/1 mile extension.
OS maps 1:25000 160 Windsor; 1:50000 186 or 175.

Start from the village hall car park at West End, SU 947 613. There is also parking near the New Engand houses, SU 936 913.

Linking walks   2★ 5❖

Hare & Hounds ☎ 01276 858161

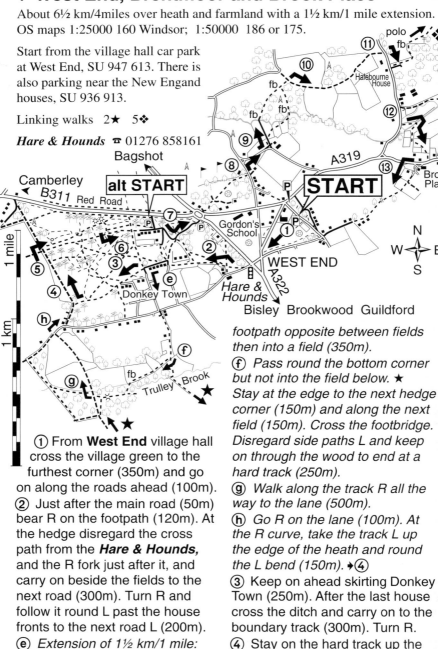

① From **West End** village hall cross the village green to the furthest corner (350m) and go on along the roads ahead (100m).
② Just after the main road (50m) bear R on the footpath (120m). At the hedge disregard the cross path from the ***Hare & Hounds,*** and the R fork just after it, and carry on beside the fields to the next road (300m). Turn R and follow it round L past the house fronts to the next road L (200m).
ⓔ *Extension of 1½ km/1 mile: Turn L down the road to the end (300m) and stay ahead on the*

footpath opposite between fields then into a field (350m).
ⓕ *Pass round the bottom corner but not into the field below. ★ Stay at the edge to the next hedge corner (150m) and along the next field (150m). Cross the footbridge. Disregard side paths L and keep on through the wood to end at a hard track (250m).*
ⓖ *Walk along the track R all the way to the lane (500m).*
ⓗ *Go R on the lane (100m). At the R curve, take the track L up the edge of the heath and round the L bend (150m). ➔④*
③ Keep on ahead skirting Donkey Town (250m). After the last house cross the ditch and carry on to the boundary track (300m). Turn R.
④ Stay on the hard track up the hill past the cross track from the ranges just over the brow (400m).

2

⑤ After the cross track (40m) turn onto the next path R. Stay on it across Brentmoor Heath (400m).

⑥ At the end of the barrows L (lumps) take the wide side path R. Don't turn off it until the cross path along the brow of the hill (120m), then go L over the rise, into the dip (100m) and up the track past the New England houses (200m).

⑦ Pass round the end of the last house, ½R and level, not steeply down. Stay on this track round a L bend (100m) to the end (250m). Go round the roundabout over the Guildford and Chobham roads (50m). Where the latter (Bagshot Road) leaves the roundabout take the footpath from the house drive under trees (150m) and diagonally over the sports field of **Gordon's School** to the wood near the L edge (200m). Walk on through the trees to the road (80m).

⑧ Go L down the road (100m) and R on the side lane (200m).

⑨ At the R bend turn L along the track between fields (150m). After the brook (Mill Bourne) stay ahead on the path curving R through the wood (350m).

⑩ At the end turn R on the horse track between fields and woods. Stay on it to the road (650m). ❖

⑪ Go R along the road. Ignore L turns after Oakfield House (100m) & Roebuck Farm Cottage (300m) but join the track L at the R curve after the next house R (100m).

⑫ Follow the track beside the L fence and cross the farm bridge at the Mill Bourne (150m). Turn R on the other side then L up between the fields (100m). Halfway to the buildings cross the field L diagon-ally to the furthest corner (150m) and go out to the road (50m).

⑬ Cross and walk R along the verge past **Brook Place** (100m). Just after the entrance turn L on the footpath into the field, soon intersecting the branching drive (50m). Just into the R drive turn L and join the track to the bend (50m). Stay ahead on the footpath mostly under trees (400m). At houses continue on the unmade road to the end (200m).

Cross the tarmac road and go R to the pond (30m). Carry on over the grass to the village hall.

The manor of Chobham included West End and was given to Chertsey Abbey as part of its early endowments. This is known from the medieval copy of a charter of about 673 - one of the first Saxon documents to bring light to the Dark Ages. The abbey wielded great influence in the vicinity for 900 years.

By the end of the 7th century charters accompanied royal grants of land. In them are written the place names of the land given and boundary marks. People with their titles and positions appear as parties and witnesses to the transaction. The arrangements reveal custom and law, and the date.

The grant of 673 was by Frithuwold who calls himself sub-king of the province of Surrey under the king of Mercia. He mentions the abbey was built by King Egbert. The lands are Chertsey, Thorpe, Egham, Chobham, Molesey amd Woodham, bounded on one side by the province of Sonning. Wulfhere, king of the Mercians, adds his sign ✚ at Thame in confirmation.

This is the document in which Surrey and the other place names first appear.

Early English Documents Vol 1 500-1042 ed Dorothy Whitlock 1955 Eyre & Spottiswoode

2 Around Bisley

About 7 km/4½ miles through heath, pasture and woods with an extension of 1½ km/1 mile or a short cut of ½ mile. OS maps 1:25000 145 + 160; 1:50000 175 Reading or 186 Aldershot.   Linking walks 1★ 3✳

Start from the car park on the village green at Bisley, SU 949 598. There is also a village car park opposite the S end of the village green, SU 949 595.

The Hen & Chickens ☎ 01483 472184   *The Fox* ☎ 01483 473175

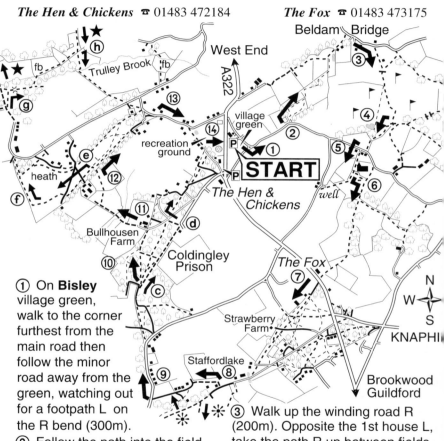

① On **Bisley** village green, walk to the corner furthest from the main road then follow the minor road away from the green, watching out for a footpath L on the R bend (300m).

② Follow the path into the field (50m) then find your way across it to the furthest corner (200m). In the next field go round the L edge and through the trees to the furthest corner (200m) then down the L edge of the next past the pond R (100m). Join the footpath between the fields and go R to the road near Beldam Bridge (200m).

③ Walk up the winding road R (200m). Opposite the 1st house L, take the path R up between fields (100m). Join the converging path and go on to the next track junction (400m).

④ Cross into the golf course R as far as the bridge (60m) then skirt the L edge (120m) and go through the next field to the road (80m).

⑤ Slightly R (30m) take the track L past Bisley Church (150m).

4

⑥ In the field after the churchyard go L along the hedge L and out at the corner (100m). Follow the path R between the fields to the main road near the **Fox** (750m).

⑦ Cross and carry on along the track into Bisley Common (150m). At the large shed after the house diverge from the fence but stay near the R boundary t   hrough the **heath** avoiding side paths (300m). Cross the drives of Strawberry Farm and the next house (300m) to the pond (100m). At the lane go on (R) until it bends L to the nursery (120m) then ahead on the track (100m). ✳

⑧ Take the side track R round the 1st house (200m). After the field R stay on the track L & R and past houses to the road (200m).

⑨ Turn R along the road past Bisley Ranges (400m). When it bends R follow the fence under the trees (300m) and the track ahead (150m). Just before the L bend, divert onto the path ahead.

ⓒ *½ mile cut: Don't fork L but stay on the straight track to the road at Coldingley Prison (500m).*

ⓓ *Turn L into the heath (100m). Turn R on the tarmac (30m) but after the side drive diverge on the path L. At the houses follow the garden boundaries ahead to the recreation ground (500m).* ➔⑭

⑩ Fork L immediately then L again (40m). Stay ahead on this path across the wood to Bullhousen Farm (350m).

⑪ Walk through the farm on the tarmac drive (70m), down the track between fields (150m) and up the L edge of the next field (100m). Halfway up bear R, cutting the corner to the stile R of the farm buildings (120m). Go straight over the next field (100m) and out into the heath.

ⓔ *Extension of 1½ km/1 mile: Just into the heath (40m), go L round the bend (40m) and over the farm drive. Carry on (150m) and cross the next drive. Swing L and R to the ranges fence (200m).*

ⓕ *Turn R and stay beside the fence to the lane (350m). Go L on the lane (300m), over the bridge and ahead on the track (100m).* ★

ⓖ *Opposite the side track L diverge R on the path under the trees to the T-junction (100m). Turn R through the wood (200m) and fork L to the footbridge (60m). Cross into the field and go R along the edge to the next field (150m) and ahead (150m).*

ⓗ *Just before the next hedge corner enter the field R and make for the bottom R corner (130m). Over the bridge (10m) turn into the field L and follow the R edge to the end (250m). Go on through the trees to the lane (120m). Just into the drive opposite, bear L across the wood (120m).* ➔⑬

⑫ Take the 1st R (20m) along the edge of the heath (400m). At the track continue ahead but fork R from the tarmac drive (200m).

⑬ At the road go R to the bend (350m) then walk out onto the recreation ground R.   Either

⑭ cross the grass to the gateway near the middle of the main road side to reach the village green (200m) or go out at the far end on the drive through the trees to the village car park (200m) and the **Hen & Chickens** (50m).

3 Pirbright and Brookwood Cemetery

About 8 km/5 miles, but can be varied; along the Basingstoke Canal, over heathland and through much of the the cemetery; fairly shady.
OS maps: 1:25000 145 Guildford; 1:50000 186 Aldershot or 175 Reading.

Start from the village green car park at Pirbright, SU 946 561. On Sundays parking is free at Brookwood Station, SU 952 569.

The Brookwood Hotel ☎ 01483 472109   *The Cricketers* ☎ 01483 473198
The Moorhen ☎ 01483 799715

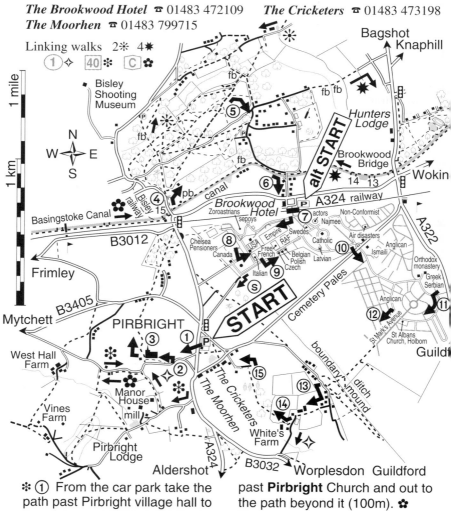

✱ ① From the car park take the path past Pirbright village hall to the main road (100m). Walk along the side road opposite (200m).

② Enter the graveyard R. See the grave of **Stanley** (granite lump) and go on along the graveyard,

past **Pirbright** Church and out to the path beyond it (100m). ✿
③ Go R along the path between fields (400m), over a road and on through the wood to the road junction (500m). Walk under the (**London to Southampton**)

6

railway bridge, ahead over the **Basingstoke Canal** at **Lock 15** (100m) and on (100m). ✳

④ Just after the two drives at the bend turn R to the footpaths. Take the R one near the house fence up through Sheets Heath (500m). Cross the narrow tarmac lane and go on along the wide track ignoring many side paths (500m).

⑤ 150m before the end, take the path which cuts the corner R to the boundary trees (120m). Join the wide track and go R (60m), ✳ over the staggered 4-way junction, down to the canal (450m). Keep on to the cart bridge (200m).

⑥ Cross and go up through **Brookwood** (200m), over the main road, to the station (80m). Via the main door pass under it to **Brookwood Cemetery** (50m).

⑦ Turn R and follow the drive parallel with the railway past the graves of Turkish airmen, sepoys and Zoroastrians (350m).

⑧ Turn L down the hill (ranks of Chelsea pensioners R) into the military area. Walk down past the Canadian area R and the American enclosure L (300m).

⑨ Follow Long Avenue L and stay on the tarmac (600m) curving R around the Najmee Baag to the exit on the road (300m).

⑩ Cross into the other part of the cemetery and stay on the main tarmac drive to the fork at the Orthodox Church and **Monastery** of St Edward (500m) then R past the Serbian Orthodox cemetery at the boundary (200m).

⑪ Keep to the circular tarmac drive until it is crossed by the long straight St Mark's Avenue (400m).

⑫ Go L along it (550m). After a deep ditch fork R to the boundary mound of Pirbright Common (60m). Slightly R, find the onward path to the tarmac lane (80m).

⑬ Go L (100m). Take the branch track R, White Lane, (50m) and continue on the footpath to the next road (150m). ✧

⑭ Go along the road L to White's Farm and take the path R, before it, into the field (100m). Turn L but diverge from the boundary to a point 100m from the L corner (150m) and go on along the path through the wood (300m).

⑮ At the end of the path turn L along the nursery track and exit via the tarmac drive to the road at *the **Cricketers*** (200m). Cross the green to the car park (200m).

Brookwood Cemetery Society gives guided tours on the first Sunday of each month and publishes a research magazine. The cemetery started as a private enterprise and is still privately owned though the military sections are now owned by the nation. In 1850 the Burials Act proscribed burials at London churches. In 1851 the London Necropolis and National Mausoleum Company obtained a private Act of Parliament enabling them to purchase 2600 acres of Woking Common. They used the 400 acres furthest from the station for the cemetery and sold the rest for building. There were 3842 funerals in 1866 making that the peak year. The company had its own line from the railway into the cemetery, its own London terminal and its own train, down 11.35 am and up 2.15 pm. Cremation was pioneered at Woking and outstripped burials after 1986 but Islamic burials have given the cemetery a new lease of life.

4 St John's to Brookwood Bridge

About 7 km/ 4¼ miles plus an extension of 2km/1½ miles; various short cuts possible; gently undulating and level beside the canal. OS maps: 1:25000 145 Guildford; 1:50000 186 Aldershot or 175 Reading.

Start fom St John's village car park, SU 979 578.

Linking walks 3✳ 14✦

The Rowbarge ☎ 01483 761618
Hunters Lodge ☎ 01483 798101

① At **St John's** village car park cross the grass, away from the Memorial Hall, to the garden hedges (50m) and follow the path round between the trees and houses to the church (300m).

② Go past the church on the road (50m) but after the churchyard turn R down the side track (100m). When it forks to houses take the path from the R fork, over the footbridge (50m) and up through the trees to the bend in the lane at houses (100m). Cross the railway footbridge (30m).

ⓔ *Extension of 2 km/1½ miles: Keep on ahead to the clubhouse (70m) then follow the drive L down round the pond (80m) and up outside the golf course. Stay ahead to the 2nd road L (400m).*

ⓕ *Turn R beween the gardens and continue on the straight path across the fairways and through the trees to the next road (800m).*

ⓖ *Just along the road R (10m) turn R on the path beside the fence of Gorse Hill (100m). At the rear stay ahead under the trees and over a fairway to a track in the next trees (80m). Follow the track ahead to the club house (600m) then R & L to the railway (100m). Don't cross. Turn L.* ✦③

③ Take the path down beside the railway into the golf course (250m). Opposite the wood L diverge from the edge to pass through the end trees to a small stone footbridge (150m). Continue in a straight line, L of the reservoir, across belts of trees and fairways (500m) then beside fields, over a footbridge (150m) and up to buildings (200m). Go L to the road (100m).

④ Walk R along the road and down under the railway (600m).

⑤ Just after the tunnel (20m) turn R up the path to the **Basingstoke Canal** (80m). Go L on the towpath under Hermitage Bridge (200m) and all the way to the next road at Brookwood Bridge (1100m). ✱
Lock 12 is just beyond the bridge. Over the bridge, a path behind the trees R of the road leads up past **Hunters Lodge** *(250m).*

⑥ Follow the path back along the other side of the canal.

ⓥ *Variant: A side path L (150m) leads up through grassland. At the first side path (80m) go R . Pass L of three ponds. Rejoin the canal.)* Continue beside the canal to the next road (1100m).

⑧ Go along the pavement R and over Hermitage Bridge (100m). Join the towpath L and follow the canal round below the railway (**London to Southampton** line) to the canal footbridge (950m).

ⓐ *Alternative: turn R on the path at the footbridge. Cross the lane and go on over a ditch (150m) and curve L along the railway (300m).*

ⓑ *At the football pitch L cross to the far corner (100m). Take the path under the trees, over a ditch to the cricket field (80m). Cross the grass to car park (150m).*

⑨ Stay on the towpath all the way to the next road at Kiln Bridge (500m). ✦ Turn R to the car park (100m) or past it and L along St John's Road to the **Rowbarge**.

The Domesday Book entry for Woking

(facsimile of the original Latin folio in Caroline minuscule script)

King William holds in lordship <u>WOCHINGES</u>. Of King Edward's revenue it was. Then it was rated for 15 hides & a half; they never paid tax. Land for 6 ploughs. In lordship is 1; 33 villeins & 9 bordars with 20 ploughs. There is a church; Osbern holds it. There is 1 mill @ 11s 4d. There are 32 acres of pasture. Woodland @ 32 pigs.
Of this land Walter son of Othere holds 3 virgates. This a certain forester held TRE & then was put out of the manor by King Edward. Nothing there now.
Value TRE & later £15 at face value; now £15 by weight,   & to the Sheriff 25s.

This is a copy of a portion of the original folio. The book itself is on display at the Public Records Office, Kew. The R and the line through WOCHINGES were highlighted in red. TRE is *Tempore Regis Edwardi* ie 1066. The Latin words are abbreviated but the script, Caroline miniscule, is legible to modern readers. The survey was initiated at the Parliament of Gloucester in 1085.

5 Chobham and Halebourne

7 km/4½ miles extending by 3½ km/2 miles to West End; mainly over pasture fields; lots of stiles. OS maps 1:25000 160 Windsor; 1:50000 175 or 186.

Start from the village car park in Chobham, SU 974 6198, or park beside the green at Burrowhill near the *Four Horseshoes*, SU 970 629.

Linking walks 1❖ 7✳ 9✿ 10❂

Hare & Hounds ☎ 01276 858161   ***The Sun Inn*** ☎ 01276 857112
Four Horseshoes ☎ 01276 857581   ***The Red Lion*** ☎ 01276 858813

❂ ① In **Chobham** walk round L to the church (200m) and take the drive opposite, between the buildings, to the cemetery (120m). Stay ahead on the path (300m).

② At the field after the nursery go ½R on the path between houses (200m), L along the road (100m), R along Clappers Lane (120m) and round the L bend (80m).

③ After the house take the path R beside the brook (40m), over the footbridge and ahead (200m) then go L on the lane past the houses (100m) and on round to the path L at the end of the field (200m).

④ Follow the path at the R edge of the fields (200m). In the field at the end, cross diagonally towards the wood far R (250m).

ⓔ *Extension: Make for the L end of the wood, find the bridge and cross the brook. At the paddocks aim diagonally R from stile to stile (200m) then follow the hedge L into the next field (80m). Cross to the corner next to the garden and exit to the road (100m). Go R along the verge opposite (150m).*

ⓕ *Just after **Brook Place** turn L through the field (50m). Cross the side drive and go on along the track (50m). At the L bend stay ahead on the footpath (400m) then on the unmade road (200m).*

ⓖ *At the tarmac road in **West End**, go R (30m), round the pond and along the L side of the village green to the corner (350m) then ahead on the roads (100m).*

ⓗ *After the main road (50m) take the path ½R (250m). At the hedge cross the path from the **Hare & Hounds** ❖ and fork R just after it. Carry on (200m) then turn R up the boundary path to the track on top (120m) (view 30m L).*

ⓘ *Follow the track R to the end (250m) and go round the roundabout over the Guildford and Chobham roads (50m). Where the Chobham road leaves the roundabout take the footpath from the drive. After the trees (150m) cross the sports field of **Gordon's School** diagonally towards the L edge (200m) and go on through the trees (100m).*

ⓙ *Walk L down the road (100m) and R on the side lane (200m).*

ⓚ *At the R bend turn L along the track between the fields (150m). After the brook (Mill Bourne) stay*

ahead on the curving path through the wood (350m).
① At the end turn R on the horse track between fields and woods. Stay on it all the way to the road (650m). Walk R along the road (100m).

⑨ At the end of the garden (40m) turn L between gardens and fields up to the next lane (350m).
⑩ Walk down the lane R to the main road (900m) and R to the green at Burrowhill ✳ and the **Four Horseshoes** (200m).

⑤ Go through the gap in the trees to the next field and aim for the L side (150m). From the bend in the brook cross the paddocks diagonally from stile to stile (300m) and follow the track out to the road (200m).
⑥ Walk along the road R (300m).
⑦ Opposite the sheds of the large roadside house, take the path beside the track into the wood and L round the edge to the footbridge (250m). Diverge from the wood across the corner of the polo field to a point 60m from the wood (100m). Cross the brook and make for the stile opposite (150m). Go through the nursery keeping to the L edge on tracks and path until near the house. Cross the ditch L to get to the road R (300m).
⑧ Walk R on the road watching out for Steep Acre Farm L (250m).

⑪ From the main road, opposite the pub, take the footpath up the grass, not the main one but the lesser path diverging R from it. Stay ahead past the end of an unmade road to Holly Cottage (200m). Beside it keep on in the same direction on the unmade road to the field hedge L (150m).
⑫ Turn R to the **Red Lion** (70m). Opposite the pub go down the un-made road (80m). Stay ahead on the path (80m), over an u-m road and along the path (60m), past the end of the tarmac, ✿ along an u-m road (100m) and path (100m).
⑬ At the next road turn R (50m) then take the footpath L between the houses. Keep on to the end of the path (400m) then follow the pavement L to the Chobham village car park (200m).

6 Chobham Common and Tank Factory

About 7 km/4½ miles through heath and woods. Many circular walks can be made on the heath. This zigzag route is an introduction passing via the nicest places, the best landmarks and several car parks. Allow time for getting lost. OS maps: 1:25000 160 Windsor; 1:50000 175 Reading.

Start from the car park at Chobham Place Wood, SU 964 642, or Longcross Car Park, SU 979 651, or Monument Car Park, SU 964 644.

Linking walks 7☆ 9★

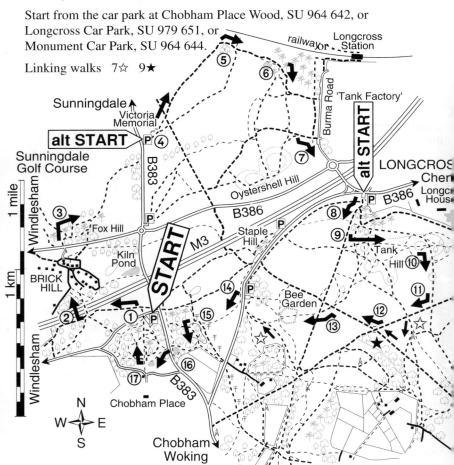

① At Chobham Place Wood cross the road from the car park. Go over the grass (30m) then turn L on the path. Keep on to the motorway footbridge R (400m).
② Cross (100m). Continue ahead through the trees (50m) then fork L to the houses of **Brick Hill** hamlet (100m). On the 1st (unmade) road

go R, round the bend up to the junction (150m) and ahead on the path between the houses (70m). Cross the next road and stay on the path to the main road (100m).
③ Slightly L continue on the other side up the path through the trees (50m) then fork R (80m) and take the next side path L curving up R

round the flank of the hillock past a side path R (150m). Go on over a rise (300m), down, up and down to the road (300m) then L on the pavement to the car park (100m).

④ From Monument Car Park go up the main track to the fork (80m). Turn back L to see the Victoria Memorial (50m) then take the L track from the fork to the 4-way junction (100m) and ahead almost straight across the highest part of **Chobham Common** (600m). The distant large building slightly R is the '**Tank Factory**'.

⑤ Carry on round the bend R and down into a valley (400m).

⑥ Rise on the other side, curving R over the brow (200m). Disregard the oblique cross path and stay ahead over lesser cross paths to a major cross track (300m).

⑦ Turn L to Burma Road (200m) and walk up it R (200m). Keep on ahead, L of the roundabout, over the motorway then round L to the junction and car park R (300m).

8 At Longcross Car Park follow the main track away from the road (100m) and fork R down the track into Chobham Common (300m).

⑨ At the 1st bulge of **Tank Hill** L climb one of the side paths L to the top of the bulge (100m). Don't turn towards the knoll on the 2nd spur of the hill. Look along the rising ridge and take the path which leads over the highest part. Just after the highest point join the cross path (400m). ★

⑩ Go R, eventually descending to the wide horse track before the power lines (350m).

⑪ Turn R, parallel with the power lines. Disregard the 1st major

cross path (150m) ☆ and continue to the next (250m).

⑫ Turn R again. Stay on this track to the oblique cross track (300m) 100m before a wider cross track.

⑬ Bear L (100m). Cross the wide track and go straight on over the **heath** to the **Bee Garden** ring mound (150m). Keep on, curving R, at the other side of the ring (100m). Turn R, not on the path along the mound but on the rising one (150m), briefly very steep, to a cross path in the trees (20m). Go L to Jubilee Mount car park (50m).

⑭ Over the road from the car park find a gap to the heath. Walk L beside the road briefly (40m) then diverge from it. Make ½R for the wooded hilltop. The paths have largely disappeared. Aim for the highest part and join the path up the edge of the wood (300m).

⑮ At the bend near the highest electricity pole take the little path into the wood, over a boundary mound to the high point (30m) and ahead briefly (40m) then turn L on the side path down through the wood to the corner of the field (150m). Turn R outside the field (80m). At the next field bear R through the trees to a pond (50m) and R of it to the road (100m).

⑯ Cross the road slightly L and find the path up the corner of the boundary mound into the wood (20m). Don't take the side path R but go on ahead near the mound up to another pond (200m).

⑰ See Chobham Place over the road then turn R on the straight path through Chobham Place Wood to the car park (300m).

7 Burrowhill Green and Chobham Common

About 7½ km/4½ miles over heathland with an extension of 1½ km/1 mile; undulating; muddy and prickly in winter; sandy and prickly in summer. OS maps: 1:25000 160 Windsor; 1:50000 175 Reading.

Start from the green at Burrowhill parking at the roadside near the *The Four Horshoes*, SU 970 629, or from Longcross Car Park, SU 979 651.

Linking walks   5✽ 6☆ 8❉ 9✦

The Four Horseshoes ☎ 01276 857581   *The Red Lion* ☎ 01276 858813

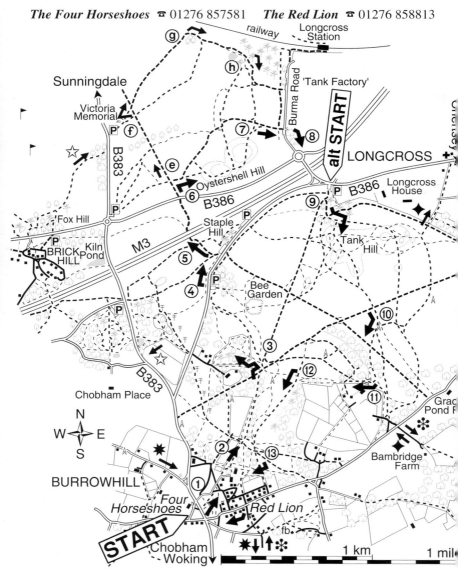

① Cross the main road opposite the ***Four Horseshoes*** (40m) and take the main path up the grass on the other side (150m). On top join the tarmac lane ahead (100m).

② At the bend go on ahead under the trees, soon beside fields. At the end of the fields (600m) stay ahead to the wide path after the power cables (200m).

③ Go R (30m) then up the 1st L (30m). Turn L on the small path which curves R up into the Jubilee Mount enclosure (50m). Pass straight up (150m), out at the top and ahead through the **heath** to Jubilee Mount car park (400m). ☆

④ Find a gap to the grass on the other side of the road and go R beside the road (250m).

⑤ Just before the car park take the curving path L down under the motorway (200m). Follow the main track ahead (300m), over the next road to a cross path (150m).

ⓔ *Extension: Stay on the same path into the valley and up to the cross path on the brow (500m).*

ⓕ *Turn L to the Y-junction(100m). Don't continue down the track to the car park but take the little path R to the memorial (30m) then return to the junction (30m). Walk away on the other track (ie fork L) to a 4-way junction (100m) and ahead, almost straight along the heath ridge (600m). Large building slightly R is the* **'Tank Factory'***.*

ⓖ *Keep on round the R curve down into the valley (400m).*

ⓗ *Go up the other side, curving R over the brow (200m). Disregard the oblique cross path and continue ahead to a major cross track (300m). Turn L.* ➔⑦

⑥ Go R to the bend (100m) then take the path up Oystershell Hill and skirt R round the top (200m). Don't take the next L but carry on and curve L down the other side to the cross path (300m). Turn R.

⑦ Keep to the wide path to Burma Road (200m).

⑧ Walk up Burma Road R to the roundabout (200m). Stay ahead, L of the roundabout, over the M3 and round L to the junction and car park R (300m).

⑨ From Longcross Car Park follow the main track away from the road (100m) and fork L (100m). Go round the bend. Don't diverge L on the horse track but carry on (70m) and take the side path R onto **Tank Hill**. ✦ Pass the 1st knoll R & the 2nd (100m) and keep on over a 3rd (200m) and down to the wide sandy horse track before the power lines (300m).

⑩ Continue ahead curving R to a pylon (100m). Disregard branch paths L and skirt R of the pylon. Ignore the L fork just after it (40m) and go on, across a wide path (100m). Follow the overgrown path down beside the wood to the the riding school fields (250m) ❇ and turn R to the bridge (40m).

⑪ Continue through the trees next to the fields (500m).

⑫ Just after the last field turn L on the heath path. Ignore all side paths and the cross track (550m) and continue to the field R with a large boundary mound (200m).

⑬ Skirt R round the mound to the houses (200m) and go on to the road at the ***Red Lion*** (80m) ✷ then R to Burrowhill Green (300m).

8 Chobham, Fishpond and Fairoaks

About 9½ km/5¾ miles over fields and through the village; impassable in wet winters at ② when the alternative route (of equal length) is less muddy. OS maps: 1:25000 160 Windsor; 1:50000 186 Aldershot.

Start from Chobham car park, SU 974 619, the fishpond car park, SU 994 635, or the verge at Fairoaks, TQ 000 622.

Linking 5✿ 7❖ 9✳ 10❀ 11❀ 13◈

The Sun Inn ☎ 01276 857112
Blubeckers ☎ 01276 857580

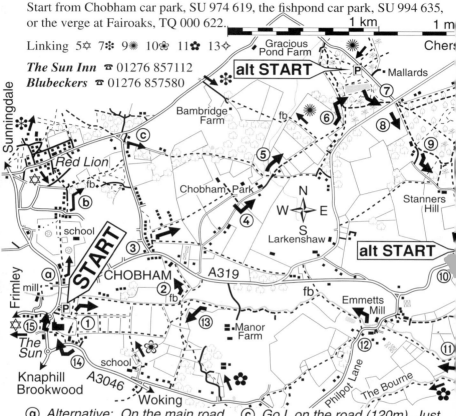

(a) *Alternative: On the main road outside Chobham village car park go R to the road junction (120m). Just after it, at the grass (50m), diverge R on the footpath, soon between sports fields (400m).*

(b) *At the housing estate go R on the road (50m) then take the path L between the houses and carry on along the (unmade) road to the T-junction (150m).❖ Turn R on the path under the trees (Little Heath) (150m). At the bridge don't fork R but keep on to the road (250m).*

(c) *Go L on the road (120m). Just before the bend turn back R along the drive to Worlds End Cottage (250m). Continue on the footpath ahead under the trees (600m). At the end of the wood follow the stream (80m) and cross the footbridge to the corner of the field at the track below the house (50m). Turn L. ➤⑤*

① In the meadows behind **Chobham** village car park go L to the stream (Mill Bourne)(200m) then R beside it. Pass the private footbridges from gardens but watch out for a public footbridge L (700m) just before a protruding bend in the R hedge.

② Cross and follow the line of trees away from the stream (50m) then bear L along the R edge to join the road near the barn (200m). Follow the verge L (100m) and turn R into Mincing Lane (30m).

③ Take the track R after the corner house and up behind the gardens (120m). Disregard the 1st footpath R but take the 2nd, along the top edge of the 2nd field. Go straight on over subsequent fields and down towards the large house, Chobham Park (600m).

④ Outside the last field go R on the track over the 1st drive and to the 2nd (80m). Go L, past the farmhouse and ahead on the track over the bridge (300m).

⑤ Take the track L of the house to the fields and carry on along the L edges (400m). ✳ After the wood L, go straight across and on at the edge to the corner (250m).

⑥ In the wood, follow the boundary track L (200m). Watch out for the pond R and take the path beside it to the end (200m). The car park is L from the end (100m). If continuing turn R. →⑦ If starting from Fishpond Car Park face the road and take the path from the R edge down between the **fishponds** (100m) & ahead.

⑦ Keep ahead on one of the small paths to the track then L to the road junction (250m). ✧

⑧ At the tracks opposite take the R path up next to the field (400m).

⑨ At the house go R to the drive. Follow it L past the large house, Stanners Hill (250m) to a junction and on down (shady path at side) to the road (500m).

⑩ Walk along the verge R (100m) then follow the Youngstroat Lane into **Fairoaks Airport** (150m). At the L bend stay ahead on the path beside fields passing the runway (500m). ❀✿ **Ottershaw Park** is the grand house visible far L over the airport.

⑪ Immediately after the stream (Mill Bourne) turn R along the bank. The path is overgrown in summer. Stay on the bank, outside the fields, to **Emmetts Mill** (600m). Continue ahead on the road (150m).

⑫ Round the S bend, before the house R, take the footpath R over the footbridges (70m) and keep on round the bend beside the stream, soon in a field. Disregard a cartbridge and a footbridge R (300m) and go on beside the stream and over the drive of Manor Farm (700m). Just after the drive (80m) cross a hedge which diverges L but stay near the stream (300m).

⑬ When the L hedge bends L, cut across the grass diagonally L to the furthest hedge corner (200m). Go into the next portion of meadow then along the L edge and round the corner (100m). Keep to the L edge of the meadow all the way to the path outside the cricket field at Chobham (600m).

⑭ Go L between the houses to the road (80m) then R (80m). Turn R on the path after the village hall to the churchyard to rejoin the road opposite the *Sun* (200m). ✿

⑮ Follow the road R through the village past ***Blubeckers*** and R at the junction (150m). The 1st and 2nd turns R lead to the village car park (100m).

9 Fishpond, Chobham Common and Longcross

About 6½ km/4 miles with a 1 km/¾ mile extension; over confusing heath and the Longcross lawns; undulating, boggy at ⑮ in winter. OS maps: 1:25000 160 Windsor; 1:50000 175 Reading.

Start from Gracious Pond Road car park, SU 994 635.

Linking walks 6★ 7✦ 8✳ 11✪ 13❖   The nearest pubs are
The Four Horseshoes ☎ 01276 857581   **The Red Lion** ☎ 01276 858813

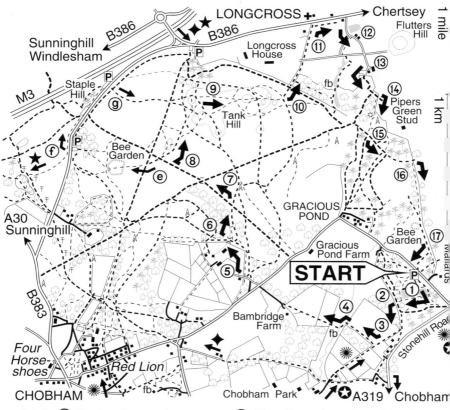

✳❖✪ ① Facing the road take the path R from the car park down between the **fishponds** (100m). Turn R along the long pond and keep on to the boundary (200m).

② Follow the boundary track L (200m) and turn R into the corner of the field. Go straight on beside the fence then over the field to the corner of the wood (200m). ✦

③ Turn R up the edge of the field beside the wood (250m).

④ Go L round the top corner of the wood (50m) then R over the footbridge. Carry on up between the fields (400m) and out along the farm drive (150m). Cross Gracious Pond Lane and go along the riding school drive opposite, almost to the house L (120m).

⑤ Turn R along the path outside the field (200m) - the boundary of **Chobham Common**. Join the track round the corner of the field L to the horse bridge (100m).

⑥ Don't cross the stream but turn R beside it (100m) then R again to the path outside the trees (20m) and L up to the wide **heath** track which crosses obliquely (150m).

⑦ Go L on the track, under the power cables (200m) and over a rise to a wide cross track (200m). *Ahead a lumpy ridge curves round on both sides. The route is onto the R arm of the ridge, Tank Hill, and along it. The extended route goes to the L arm first.*
Stay on the track ahead (300m). Turn off at the oblique cross path 100m before the next major track.

★ⓔ *Extension: Bear L to the wide track (100m) and go straight on over the heath (150m) and* **Bee Garden**, *curving R to the far edge (100m). Turn R, not on the path along the mound, but the uphill one (150m) which steepens to a cross path in the trees (20m). Go L to Jubilee Mount car park (50m).*

ⓕ *Over the road find a gap to the heath and walk R beside the road (300m). Carry on past the car park and find a path up L in the pines to Staple Hill. Stay on the ridge to the next car park's exit (250m).*

ⓖ *Cross the road and go straight down through the heath (400m), over the wide track and up onto the L knoll of the hill (100m).* ➔ⓖ

⑧ Take the path back R up round the flank of a small hill L and fork R on one of the steeper paths to reach the knoll on top of the 2nd spur of Tank Hill (500m).

⑨ From the knoll, look along the rising ridge and take the path which leads over the highest point. Just after the top is a cross path (400m). Slightly R take the small onward path down the end of the ridge converging on a wider path below (200m).

⑩ Follow the main path down to the boundary track (80m) where a path passes through the fence to the wood. Go through the wood (100m) and on along the L fence, over the drive of Longcross House (100m) almost to the road near **Longcross** Church (100m).

⑪ Walk R along the edge of the park near the road (300m).

⑫ From the main gates take the drive back across the park, round L after the pond and over crossroads to the next buildings (350m).

⑬ Bear R to the wood (70m) and go on along the winding horse track in the trees (200m). Don't take the wide branch track R.

⑭ At the next gateway go R along the fence (100m). When the fence bends L, continue ahead, L of the **barrow** (100m), under the power cables (100m) and on (70m).

⑮ On the next crossing track go L and down (200m). When it bends R, continue on the footpath ahead curving L to mound & ditch at the boundary of the Common (200m).

⑯ Don't cross the boundary. Go R. Stay near boundary through the trees. At a slight bend in the ditch the earthworks are the lesser **Bee Garden** (hidden by vegetation in summer)(400m). Keep on along the boundary path (200m).

⑰ On a little rise the path bends R to the road and car park (200m).

10 **Horsell Common, Chobham & Emmetts Mill**

About 8 km/5 miles with a shorter version 2½ km/1½ miles less; over fields and heath. OS maps 1:25000 160 Windsor; 1:50000 186 Aldershot.

Start from the western car park on Horsell Common, TQ 001 604, or from the village car park in Chobham, SU 974 619.

Linking walks 5🟊 8🕸 11🌸 12✳ 13☆ 14🟊

The Sun Inn ☎ 01276 857112   *Blubeckers* ☎ 01276 857580

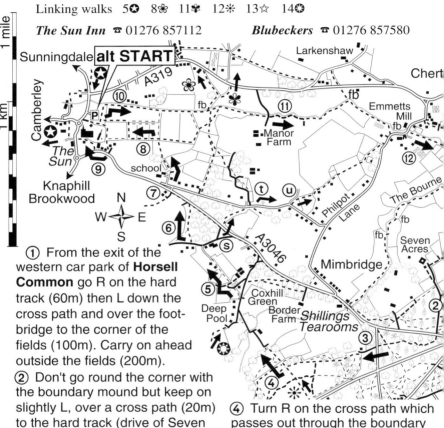

① From the exit of the western car park of **Horsell Common** go R on the hard track (60m) then L down the cross path and over the footbridge to the corner of the fields (100m). Carry on ahead outside the fields (200m).

② Don't go round the corner with the boundary mound but keep on slightly L, over a cross path (20m) to the hard track (drive of Seven Acres) and L to the road (200m). Opposite, take the horse track into the trees. It curves R, parallel with the next road (100m), then bends away from it, winding across the Common to another road (300m).

③ Cross and go along the track, opposite, to Bourne Place (100m). Continue past the house on the horse track through the Common disregarding all side paths (500m).

④ Turn R on the cross path which passes out through the boundary nearby (40m). Carry on between fields (100m). In the next field join the track ahead, round the S-bend over the stream (**Bourne**)(200m) to houses (150m) then R (100m).

⑤ After the 2nd house turn L into the nursery at the field gate and follow the R hedge (100m). The nursery plots disrupt the line of the right of way and it is best to turn L to the parallel hedge then R to the

20

track outside the nursery (50m). Over the track, slightly R, the path resumes the original line between the fields (200m). At the houses (Milford Farm) keep on to the end of the tarmac drive (150m).

(S) *Shorter version: Turn R along the unmade road (100m) and, at the large house, fork L to the road (100m). Cross to the horse track opposite and carry on through the trees to the next road (250m).*

(t) *Walk R along the road (250m).*

(u) *At the R bend enter the field next to the drive and follow the L edge. When the drive bends L keep on at the edge of the fields (200m) and skirt round the antisocial garden fences (150m). Cross the next field slightly R (150m). Over the track continue ahead between the paddocks to the road (200m).*

Go L along the road and round the S-bend to the bridge (200m). ➔⑫

⑥ Go L (60m). Between the 1st & 2nd houses watch out for the path R through the trees and follow it to the road (300m).

⑦ Walk along the pavement L to the road junction (100m) and cross to cul-de-sac part of the side road. Just after the junction (50m) turn R on the tarmac drive at the edge of the school site (100m). Carry on along the edge of the

sports area (100m) and across the middle of the next field (100m).

⑧ In the next field turn L. Keep to the edge of the meadows all the way to the path outside the cricket field at **Chobham** (300m).

⑨ Go L between the houses to the road (80m) then R (80m). Turn R on the path after the village hall to the churchyard to rejoin the road opposite the *Sun* (200m). ✪ Follow the road R through the village past **Blubeckers** and R at the road junction (150m). Take the 1st or 2nd turnings R to the village car park (100m). ❀

⑩ In the meadows behind the village car park go L to the stream, Mill Bourne, (200m) and R beside it. Ignore a footbridge L near the bend of the R hedge (700m). ✿ Keep on along the stream (400m).

⑪ Cross the drive of Manor Farm and stay beside the stream. Eventually the path turns R and crosses footbridges to the road (750m). Go L on the road round the S-bend to the bridge (150m).

⑫ Don't cross the road bridge at **Emmetts Mill** but turn R beside it and continue on the bank of the Mill Bourne to the horse track crossing it (600m). ☆

⑬ Turn R and cross the next stream (Bourne) (150m). Stay on the path ahead to the vehicle track in Horsell Common (400m). ✳

⑭ Cross the track and bear L on the path through the **heath** to the little pond (250m).

⑮ Level with the pond turn R. Go round the L bend (60m) then stay ahead to the main track under the trees (300m). ✪ The car park is R (150m).

11 **Fairoaks, the Bourne and Mimbridge**

About 8 km/5 miles, mainly through meadows and woodland. OS maps
1:25000 160 Windsor; 1:50000 186 Aldershot.

Start from Fairoaks Airport; park on the verge opposite Youngstroat Lane,
TQ 000 622, or ask to park at Shillings Tearooms, SU 991 606.

Linking walks   8✿   9⊙   10❀   12★   13✳   14✪

Fairoaks Coffee Shop 01276 485897
Shillings Tearooms 01276 855030

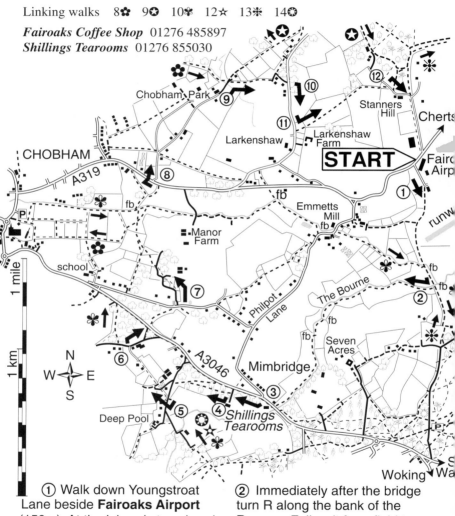

① Walk down Youngstroat
Lane beside **Fairoaks Airport**
(150m). At the L bend stay ahead
on along the path between fields.
Ottershaw Park is visible far L
over the runway (500m). ❀★⊙
Cross the 1st stream (Mill Bourne)
and carry on to the 2nd (200m).

② Immediately after the bridge
turn R along the bank of the
Bourne. Follow it from field to
field (1000m) then cross the
footbridge and carry on on the
other bank along the field to the
road at **Mimbridge** (600m)
opposite *Shillings Tearooms*.

③ Cross the road and walk R along the pavement, past Philpot Lane (100m) and ahead (200m).

④ Turn L into the drive of Border Farm but watch out for the side path R in the trees (40m). Follow the path through the trees (300m). Join the converging path and carry on to the hard track near the nursery gateway (100m).

⑤ Turn L along the hard track to the 1st house R (120m). Just before the house turn R at the field gate into the nursery and follow the R hedge (100m). The nursery plots disrupt the line of the right of way and it is best to turn L to the parallel hedge then R to the wide track outside the nursery (50m). Over the track, slightly R, the path continues on the original line between fields (200m). At the houses (Milford Farm) keep on to the end of the drive (150m). ✿

⑥ Turn R along the unmade road (100m) and, at the large house, fork L to the road (100m). Cross to the track opposite and carry on under telegraph wires through the trees to the next road (250m).

⑦ Cross, slightly R, and take the drive of Manor Farm round L & R bends to a major track junction (250m). Follow the L track round the trees watching out for a stile at the corner of a field L (100m). Cross the field, diverging from the track to the middle of the opposite edge (80m). Cross the next small field aiming slightly L for the corner (60m). In the next field cut across the corner to the middle of the R edge (200m). ✿ In the next go straight out from the fence, approximately parallel with the R

hedge. When the hedge bends R carry on ahead and cross the footbridge over the Mill Bourne (200m). Follow the line of trees ahead. Disregard a side path L and carry on to the road (200m).

⑧ Go L along the verge (50m) and cross into the drive of Chobham Park. At the fork (200m) stay on the main drive R to Chobham Park Farm (500m). At the farmhouse continue along the track (150m). ❍

⑨ After the bridge go R on the path along the garden hedge then between fields to the houses in the trees (300m). Follow the main track L & R to the road (200m).

⑩ Walk past the houses along the road R (300m). In the first small field L watch out for a path, 30m before the Larkenshaw drive.

⑪ Cross the little field into the larger one beyond (80m). Walkers tend to follow the L edge around but the right-of-way is straight across to the top edge at a point 30m from the L corner (300m). Continue ahead at the L edge of the next field past the trees and round R up towards the wood (250m). At the top corner exit to the tarmac drive (30m). ✳

⑫ Go down the drive R past the large house, Stanners Hill, to the drive junction (200m). Carry on down. There is a shady path R of the drive (400m). At the road turn R to the parking place.

Duckweed, *Lemna sulca*, makes ponds look bright green and solid. It is an abberant flowering plant. Grow on window sills for infants to count.

x1

12 Horsell Common and Mimbridge

About 7 km/4½ miles; mainly through heath and woodland; flat.
OS maps 1:25000 145 + 160; 1:50000 186 Aldershot.

Start from Horsell Common west car park, TQ 001 604.

Linking walks   10❋   11★   13❊   14★

The Plough 01483 714105   ***Shillings*** 01276 855030

① From **Horsell Common** west car park, go along the hard track towards the road (100m). Halfway, take the side path ½R and cross the road junction to Cheapside (100m). Follow the lane beside the trees. Stay ahead to the ***Plough*** (600m).

② Along the road L after the pub (150m) diverge R on the path through the trees, across a side road and on to houses (200m). Continue ahead on tarmac (200m). At the end of the tarmac stay on the track ahead to the R bend (100m).

③ Go on round the bend to the main road (100m). Cross to Horsell Common and take the L path ahead to the far boundary (350m). Carry on between fences (100m). In the next field join the track ahead and pass round the S-bend over the stream (**Bourne**) (200m) to the next houses at Deep Pool (150m). ❋★ Follow the track R past houses, into the trees (200m).

④ Just before the nursery drive L take the horse track R through the trees (100m) and fork R on the side track which ends at the drive of Border Farm (300m) near the road in **Mimbridge** (40m). Follow the pavement R past the side road & ***Shillings Tearooms*** to the Mim Bridge (300m). Cross the road.

ⓐ *Shady alternative: After the Mim Bridge (40m) find the horse track under the trees L into Horsell Common and diverge from the road to the drive of the farm (300m). Cross and go on along the track (200m). When it bends*

to the last house stay ahead on the path through the wood to another track - the drive of Seven Acres (150m).

ⓑ *Turn L (30m) then fork R on the R hard track beside the field (120m). Opposite the house turn R. Disregard side turns and snake round several houses. After the fields join the perimeter track of Horsell Common (500m). Just along the hard track, from the bend L (30m) take the path R.* →⑦

⑤ Just before the bridge enter the field L and follow the bank of the Bourne to the end of the field (600m). Cross the footbridge and carry on along the bank from field to field to the horse track crossing the Bourne (1000m). ❋

⑥ Walk along the horse track R to the perimeter hard track at the corner of Horsell Common (400m). Cross to the path slightly L.

⑦ Follow the path into the **heath** (100m). Turn L on the 1st cross track (not back L to the perimeter).

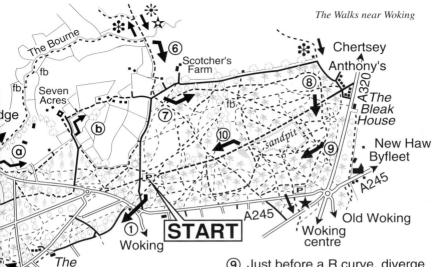

② The Plough

Stay on this horse track (250m) and fork L. Keep on to open heath and ahead near the L edge to the little pond L and trees at the end (750m) then round R to a cross track (200m), near **Anthony's**.

⑧ Go on under trees (120m) to another cross track. Stay ahead disregarding side paths (150m). ★

⑨ Just before a R curve, diverge ½R on the side path. Fork R and cross another path (100m) to the corner of the **sandpit** in the trees (20m). Go L all the way along outside the sandpit (650m).

⑩ At the far end of the sandpit, carry on in the same direction on the parallel, wide, straight track, R of the pond, to Horsell Common west car park (600m).

Commons are usually open to the public for air and exercise but are not owned by the public or by the nation. They are remnants of land called *waste* in early documents which was not ploughed for crops but used for grazing, firewood, peat cutting, building materials, etc. As the population became denser the waste was divided between communities who marked boundaries with mounds or hedges in medieval times. The land now belonged to the lord of the manor and commoners; they could use it for themselves but not work it for private profit or sell it.

For enterprise there was a tendency from the Middle Ages onwards for shared arable land to be parcelled by agreement into private farms and much of the waste was taken up in the process. If commoners resisted, they were overcome, later on, by private Acts of Parliament. Only village greens and the least useful commons survived. Surrey has large commons because of poor soils and extensive heaths.

In the 20th century commons lost sight of their commoners; a commoner might have the right to graze two cows but was not allowed to fence them and would not want to herd them; coal replaced peat and firewood; &c. By default, lords of the manor became the only visible owners and were able to dispose of commons. In Surrey they sold to boroughs, builders, the Army, preservation societies and the Forestry Commission. There are still a few commoners with registered rights.

The Common Lands of England & Wales W G Hoskins & L Dudley Stamp 1963 Collins

13 Horsell Common and Fairoaks

About 8 km/5 miles, around Fairoaks Airport, through pinewoods and over heath with a 1 km/¾ mile extension. Horsell Common and Stanners Hill have numerous paths which can be explored but the route takes you via the main landmarks. OS maps: 1:25000 160 + 145; 1:50000 186 Aldershot.

Start at Horsell Common main car park near Six Ways, TQ 011 603, or at Monument Lane car park, TQ 015 597, or at Fairoaks Airport, parking on the verge opposite Youngstroat Lane, TQ 000 622.

Linking 8✧ 9❖ 10☆ 11✳ 12✿ 14✲ 19❀

The Bleak House 01483 760613
Fairoaks Coffee Shop 01276 485897

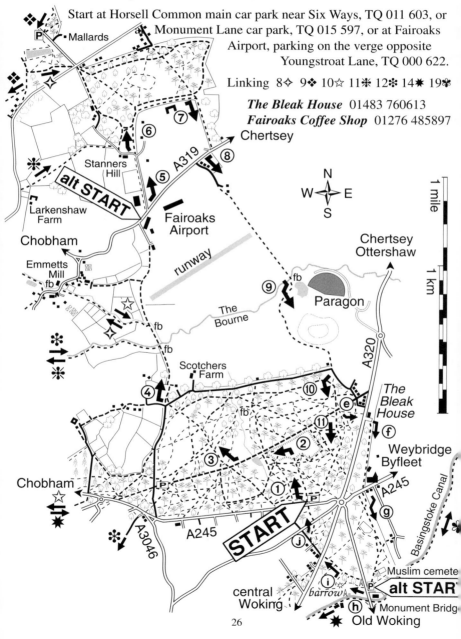

① Follow the footpath from the car park entrance straight across **Horsell Common** and into the **sandpit** (400m).

② Turn L and make your way to the narrow end of the pit (200m). Outside join the parallel straight track and continue ahead, R of the pond (100m) and on (150m). ☆❋

③ Turn R on the 1st substantial side path. Ignore the many side paths. Don't fork R (200m) but keep on past a tiny pond (200m) to the boundary track at the corner of the Common (250m).

④ Continue, opposite, on the soft bridleway over two streams, the **Bourne** (500m) ❋ and Mill Bourne (200m).✧ The grand house far R across **Fairoaks Airport** is **Otter-shaw Park**. At the end (500m) stay ahead on the drive (200m).

⑤ At the road go R (100m) then up the house drive L. A shady path runs beside it L (400m). ❖

⑥ At the fork after Stanyards Farm, take the path between the branches. Ascend under trees and make your way R to the boundary. Follow the path beside gardens across Stanners Hill and on outside the field R (700m).

⑦ At the end of the field take the path R beside it down to the road (350m). Go R on the road (200m).

⑧ At the houses, turn L into the track (Bonsey's Lane). When this bends L to the farm (250m) keep on beside the airfield and down to the Bourne (800m).

⑨ Over the footbridge, stay on the curving path past the **Paragon** building L, up round the hillock and down to the house at the edge of Horsell Common (300m).

⑩ Continue ahead (50m) then take the path through the trees R (50m) and turn L on the **heath** horse track. Pass over the 1st cross track (150m) and continue to the 2nd (120m) near **Anthony's**. Either ⑪ Stay on the path ahead all the way to the car park (600m). or ⓔ *Extend the route by ¾ mile/ 1 km: At the 2nd cross track don't continue ahead but turn L to the next path junction (20m). Turn R (15m) then branch ½L straight to the road (traffic visible) and cross to the **Bleak House** (150m).*

ⓕ *From the pub car park take the path R along the boundary of the Common to the next road near Woodham Church (500m).*

ⓖ *Keep on along the path, opposite, curving R from the boundary (100m). On the crossing path from the road go L past the corner of the boundary mound R (200m). Just after the mound fork R. Join the converging path (100m) and continue past the* **Muslim cemetery** *to the car park at the road (250m). Walk up onto the Monument Bridge over the* **Basingstoke Canal** *(50m).* ❋❀

ⓗ *Return along the pavement on the other side of the road looking for a path L opposite the car park but before the pylon (70m). Follow the path across the Common and over the* **barrow** *(200m).*

ⓘ *Just after the middle of the barrow (20m) turn R through the trees to the long straight path (100m). Go L to the road (150m) over it and along Carlton Road to Woodham House (150m).*

ⓙ *Take the path R across two roads to the car park (250m).*

14 Woking and the Basingstoke Canal

About 9½ km/6 miles through woods and heath and along the towpath in Woking.   OS maps 1:25000 145 + 160; 1:50000 186 Aldershot.

Start from Horsell Common main car park near Six Ways, TQ 011 603, or the West car park, TQ 001 604, or from Littlewick Recreation Ground, SU 981 592.

The Bridge Barn ☎ 01483 763642   *The Fox & Flowerpot* ☎ 01483 228920

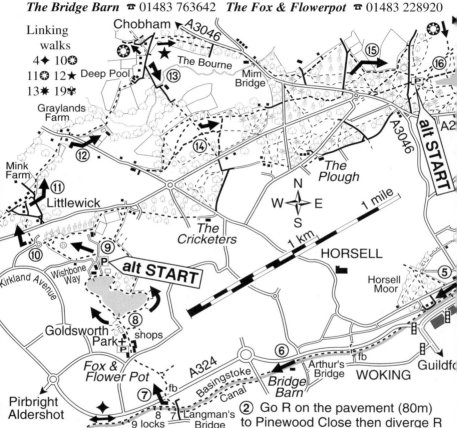

① Near Six Ways take the path over the road from the car park exit, through **Horsell Common**, (100m). Cross the next road and go on to Woodham House (120m) then L to the main road (120m).

ⓔ *¼ mile extension: Cross. Go on through the trees (300m) and R on the road over the canal (120m).*

ⓕ *Drop to the towpath and go L to the next bridge (650m).* ✦④

② Go R on the pavement (80m) to Pinewood Close then diverge R on the path in the trees (150m).

③ Just after the next road (50m), bear L on the side path. Keep on over a ditch (150m) and disregard all side turns (200m). Climb to the road to cross the canal (100m). Drop to the towpath and turn L.

④ Go on to the next road (500m).

⑤ Cross the canal and continue on the other side through **Woking** (450m), under the next road and

28

on to Arthur's Bridge near the **Bridge Barn** pub (700m).

⑥ Stay on the towpath, under the next road (300m) to the bridge at the first lock (No 7) (500m). ✦

⑦ Turn R, not down the track but up the diverging walkway over the

Old Woking road and ahead to the next road at **Goldsworth Park** (500m). Keep on ahead past the **Fox & Flowerpot**, along the shop fronts into the park and ahead to the pond (300m).

⑧ Follow the path round to the children's play area at other end of the pond, L (500m) or R (600m).

⑨ Walk away from the pond past the buildings ★ and cut straight over the grass and football field into the far L corner (500m).

⑩ Exit L. Cross the road circle (50m) and turn R on the walkway beside Weasdale Court to the main road (100m). Cross to the footpath in the trees and keep on to the track (100m), then slightly L and along the side track to the end (100m).

⑪ Turn R along the garden hedges (80m). Cross the S-bend at the next track (Mink Farm drive)

to the field and continue along R edges in the trees to the large field (100m). Keep on to cross the bridge at the far R corner (200m) and go out to the road (100m).

⑫ Cross the road and go R to the 1st field (30m). Follow the path round the R edge, soon diverging from the road (200m). In the next, narrow field cross the footbridge ½L (50m). Go straight over to the edge of the field (30m) and ahead between two fields (150m). In the next field follow the fence R to the house (100m). Join the track and go R round the house (100m). ☺★

⑬ Turn back R on the side track past the pond to the **Bourne** bridge (150m). Keep on round the S-bend and along the edge of the field (150m). Don't turn L with the track but go out at the corner then between fences (150m) and into Horsell Common.

⑭ Start along the path ahead (40m) but take the cross path L at the edge of the heath and through the trees to Bourne Place (500m). Go on along the drive (100m), over the road and through the trees on the winding path (400m).

⑮ Cross the road into the hard track opposite (Seven Acres drive) (30m). Disregard the small paths R near the road but take the 3rd to the corner of fields (200m). Stay ahead outside the fields until the next corner (200m) then bear R over the footbridge up to the hard track near the W car park (100m).

⑯ Walk through the car park and on along the the broad track ✱ until past the pond R (700m).

⑰ Take the next path R and skirt round outside the **sandpit** (200m).

⑱ At the cross path from the 2nd spur of the sandpit turn R to the main car park (200m).

15 Old Woking to Send Church

About 8 km/5 miles with a 1 km/¾ mile extension; a flat walk in the Wey valley; may be impassable in wet winters. The Navigation towpath can be used for short cuts. OS maps 1:25000 145 Guildford; 1:50000 186 Aldershot.

Start from Old Woking car park, TQ 018 569, or a parking spot near Send crossroads, TQ 027 553.

Linking walks   16✿   17✿   18★   ⑩ ✳

The White Hart ☎ 01483 763202   *The New Inn* ☎ 01483 762736

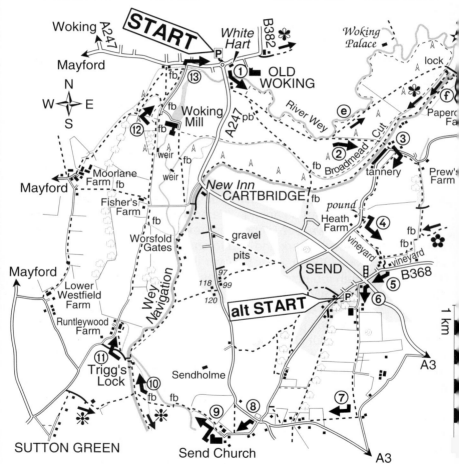

✳① Opposite **Old Woking** car park, follow Broadmead Road over the River **Wey** to the end of the houses L (150m) then diverge L on the track to the fields (100m).

Don't take the R fork to the pillbox. Either join the winding river bank path L or stay on the main path skirting the meanders to the fork after the 2nd river loop (800m).✿★

(e) *Extension of 1km/¾ mile to* **Papercourt** *Lock: Fork L along the meadow and cross the Navigation (600m).*

(f) *Go R along the towpath to the next bridge (700m).* ↳(3)

(2) Fork R towards the L end of the long building, Send Tannery, crossing the **Broadmead** Cut and the **Wey Navigation** (300m).

(3) Walk along the path beside the Send Tannery buildings (50m) and ahead on the lane (50m). Just before the house drive L pass R through the hedge into the corner of the field and follow the path at the R edge until a concrete track crosses the lane (500m). Join the lane briefly. See the pound R, and enter the next gate L (50m).

(4) Walk round the shed and on at the R edge of the field (100m). Go round the corner and on along the edge past the **vineyard** to the next corner, near houses, (250m) then R to the road (100m).

(5) Walk R, over **Send** crossroads (150m) and on (50m).

(6) Turn L up Bush Lane to the school (150m). At the school gate turn L outside the fence and keep on at the edge of the field (400m) then on a tarmac track (60m). At the bend continue through the field ahead initially beside a hedge then over to the converging edge near buildings (250m).

(7) Don't join the lane but turn R at a right angle on the other footpath (often obscure) across the fields eventually joining the road at the corner next to the garden (300m). Go R along the road down to the junction (200m) and ahead to the staggered crossroads (60m).

(8) Walk down the lane L to **Send Church** (250m).

(9) In the churchyard walk right round the church and out at the gate opposite the house (150m). Follow the path L around the garden (50m) and go on along the footpath beside the ditch through the fields to the footbridge over the River Wey (500m). Keep on along the bank until the river curves R (100m) then ahead to the visible bridge over the invisible Wey Navigation. Aim slightly L of the straight line to find the low bridge over a ditch (200m). ✳

(10) Don't cross the Navigation here but walk along the towpath R to Trigg's Lock (250m).

(11) Cross the canal and start along the track (80m). Enter the 1st field R and cross diagonally to the far end of the buildings L (250m) then take the concrete track away from Runtleywood Farm over the ditch and keep on along the L edges of the fields to the drive at Fisher's Farm (800m). Enter the field ahead and carry on at the R edge (350m). Go through the thicket under power cables (100m) and on along the next field (100m).

(12) Don't cross the footbridge over the stream R, but go L to the gap in the hedge then converge on the stream R to the next footbridge (150m). Don't cross it but keep on beside the stream and exit from the corner to the drive of **Woking Mill** (300m).

(13) Walk R along the main road (see the mill through the trees R) to the road the junction (250m) near the car park and ***White Hart***.

16 Old Woking, Newark and Cartbridge

A Wey Navigation walk. About 6½ km/4 miles, flat but boggy in winter, or a drier extended version of 11 km/6¾ miles with gentle undulation; half shady. OS maps 1:25000 145 Guildford; 1:50000 186 Aldershot + 187 Dorking.

Start from Old Woking car park, TQ 018 569, or Newark Bridges car park, TQ 039 573.

Linking walks
15❋ 17★ 18❋
24◇ ⑪❋

The White Hart
☎ 01483 763202
The New Inn
☎ 01483 762736
The Seven Stars
☎ 01483 225128

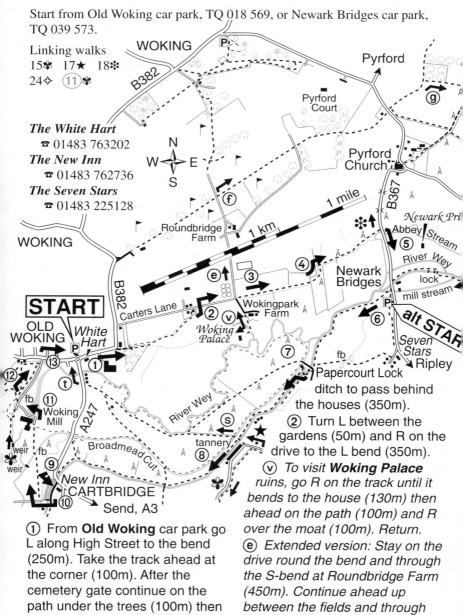

ditch to pass behind the houses (350m).

② Turn L between the gardens (50m) and R on the drive to the L bend (350m).

ⓥ To visit **Woking Palace** ruins, go R on the track until it bends to the house (130m) then ahead on the path (100m) and R over the moat (100m). Return.

ⓔ Extended version: Stay on the drive round the bend and through the S-bend at Roundbridge Farm (450m). Continue ahead up between the fields and through the golf course (250m).

① From **Old Woking** car park go L along High Street to the bend (250m). Take the track ahead at the corner (100m). After the cemetery gate continue on the path under the trees (100m) then straight over the field beside the

(f) *Watch out for the cross path under trees and follow it R, over a drive (600m), up beside the wood (350m) and on to the road (350m). Slightly L continue opposite on the path to the wood (300m).* ✻

(g) *Take the side path R to the bottom of the field (300m). A little R go on in the same line between fields then on the road (450m).* ✧

Just into the drive of Pyrford Place (50m) join the path in the field R. Go on beside the drive (120m).

(h) *In the next field cross diagonally to the gate R (100m). Exit and keep on ahead beside the ditch (100m), then on the other side, to the end of the wood (200m). Go over the golf course slightly L to the footbridge (100m) and on to the end of the channel (100m). Turn L to the trees at the edge (150m) and go out to the Navigation then R (200m). Cross at Walsham Gates (100m).* ★

(i) *Follow the towpath R, crossing at the next lock (900m). The ruin R is Newark Abbey. Keep on to the road at Newark Mill (300m).* ➜(6)

(3) At the bend take the footpath ahead twixt fence & ditch (350m) and through the next field (150m).

(4) Cross the ditch at the end (before a pylon) and turn L. Follow the ditch round the bend L into the next field (120m) then turn R to the next pylon (150m) and keep on near the ditch, R, to join the road at the bridge (300m). ✻

(5) Cross to the pavement. Follow the road R over the Abbey Stream then the River **Wey** (200m) then the **Wey Navigation** (100m). ★

(6) Opposite **Newark Mill** house take the path to the meadows. Cross the mill leat (100m) and carry on along the river bank to **Papercourt** Lock (700m).

(7) Cross the bridge and continue on the other side to the next footbridge (700m). ✻

(s) *Short cut, saving 2km/1¼ mile: Turn R on the footpath over the meadows to the river (300m) and keep on (L) to the road (900m). Turn R to High Street (150m).*

(8) Go on along the towpath opposite Send Tannery. Ignore the next footbridge (700m) and keep on to Cartbridge (800m).

(9) After the road bridge climb the steps and cross the water towards the **New Inn** (100m).

(10) Walk along the track between the pub and the Navigation (150m) then cross the footbridge R and a drive to the cart track (50m). Go L (50m) and enter the corner of the meadow R. Diverge from the R edge to the footbridge over **Broadmead** Cut (300m) and keep on to the R edge of the large building, **Woking Mill** (250m).

(11) Join the drive ahead (40m) and go L round the building (150m).

(12) Don't follow the next bend in the drive but go on through the trees and over the footbridge (50m) then follow the ditch R and exit at the end (350m).

(13) Walk along High Street R to the road junction (250m) near the **White Hart** and car park.

17 Ripley, Papercourt and Newark Priory

About 7 km/4¾ miles with an extension of 1½ km/1 mile; a flat Wey Navigation walk with many possible variations; few stiles; little shade. OS maps 1:25000 145 Guildford; 1:50000 186 Aldershot + 187 Dorking.

Start at Newark Bridges car park, TQ 039 573, 100m S of the bridge with traffic lights, or at Ripley Green car park, TQ 053 571, off Ripley High Street via the drive next to the *Half Moon*.

Linking walks   15✿ 16★ 18✳ 24☆ 25✪ ⑪✿

The Half Moon ☎ 01483 224380
The Talbot ☎ 01483 225188
The Anchor ☎ 01483 211721
The Seven Stars ☎ 01483 225128

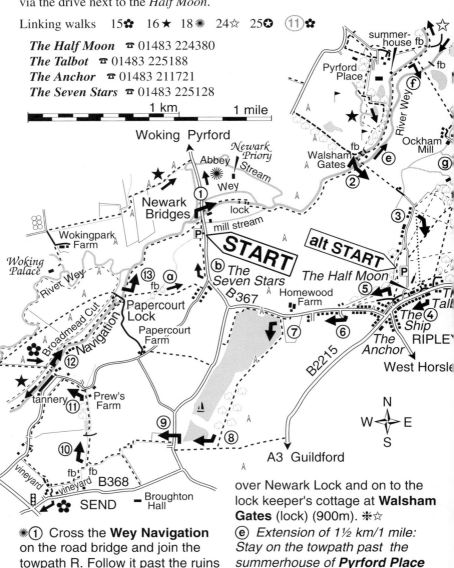

✳① Cross the **Wey Navigation** on the road bridge and join the towpath R. Follow it past the ruins of **Newark Priory** far L (400m),

over Newark Lock and on to the lock keeper's cottage at **Walsham Gates** (lock) (900m). ✳☆

ⓔ *Extension of 1½ km/1 mile: Stay on the towpath past the summerhouse of **Pyrford Place** (600m) and ahead (200m).*

(f) *100m before the next foot-bridge (Pigeon House Bridge) turn R along the footpath over the river. At the track continue to* **Ockham Mill** *(700m). Go L over the mill tail and on along the lane (150m).* ✪

(g) *At the crossing path turn off R, curving round into the wood (400m). After the 2nd horse bridge continue ahead and fork R.* ➜③

② After seeing the lock, return over the sluice gates and take the footpath straight on between the fields then the track ahead past a house to the bend (600m). Cross the grass diagonally R.

③ Cross Ripley Green making for the distant row of buildings which is **Ripley**. Skirt the cricket field to the clubhouse with clock and exit between the buildings to the main road opposite the *Talbot* (600m).

④ Turn R along the High Street, past the *Half Moon* and side lane (150m). (The *Anchor* and church are further on).

⑤ Opposite the *Ship* pass between the shops R to the Green (50m) and turn L on one of the paths to the narrow extremity of the grass and the road (300m).

⑥ Follow Newark Lane out of the village past Dunsborough House twin lodges and on (400m).

⑦ At the end of the 1st field go L through the hedge to the gravel pit lake and L along the water's edge (500m). After the pylon bear L through the wood. Keep on to the field (500m).

⑧ Join the footpath along the top fence to the road R (300m).

⑨ Cross the lane to the housing estate slightly R (50m). Enter the gateway R of it, and follow the footpath behind the houses into the field (150m). Keep on at the L edge of the field and round the zigzags (500m). ✿

⑩ At the T-junction turn R along the ditch between fields (150m) then cross and walk on the other side almost to the lane (350m).

⑪ Go L at the edge of the field (150m). At the next corner join the lane to the bend at Send Tannery (30m). Go down the footpath at the R end of the building and over the Navigation footbridge (50m).★

⑫ Follow the tow path R (700m). Across the meadows L see **Old Woking** church & part of **Woking Palace** - an isolated grey building.

⑬ At **Papercourt** Lock re-cross the Navigation. Either turn L and carry on along the bank to Newark Bridges (900m) or

(a) *Go straight over the field to the footbridge (200m) and on in the same line then between houses to the* **Seven Stars** *(300m).*

(b) *Turn L to return to Newark Bridges, along the R verge then the path under the trees L.*

Tufted Ducks increased in population during the 20th century. The winter numbers are augmented by migrants from the north. The drake is black with a white patch and dangling crest; the duck is dark brown. They are smaller than Mallards. The drake of the rarer Goldeney looks similar in the distance but has a very long head.

A3 Ockam M25

18 Newark Mill to Pyrford Lock

About 8 km/5 miles but can be shorter or longer; across water meadows and fields and along the Wey Navigation; almost level.
OS maps 1:25000 145 Guildford; 1:50000 186 + 187.

Start from Newark Bridges car park, TQ 039 573, or from Pyrford Lock public car park, TQ 053 593.

Linking walks 15✫ 16✤ 17✳
19✿ 24✳ 25❂ (11)✿

The Seven Stars ☎ 01483 225128
The Anchor ☎ 01932 342507

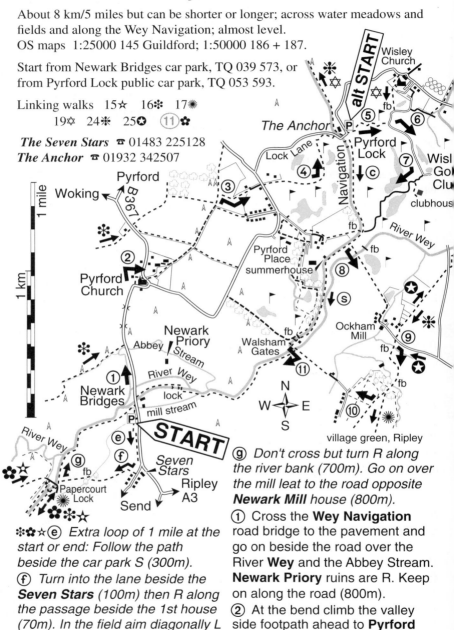

✤✿✫ⓔ *Extra loop of 1 mile at the start or end: Follow the path beside the car park S (300m).*
ⓕ *Turn into the lane beside the* ***Seven Stars*** *(100m) then R along the passage beside the 1st house (70m). In the field aim diagonally L for the footbridge (near trees) then in the same line for the bridge at* **Papercourt** *Lock (500m).*

ⓖ *Don't cross but turn R along the river bank (700m). Go on over the mill leat to the road opposite* ***Newark Mill*** *house (800m).*
① Cross the **Wey Navigation** road bridge to the pavement and go on beside the road over the River **Wey** and the Abbey Stream. **Newark Priory** ruins are R. Keep on along the road (800m).
② At the bend climb the valley side footpath ahead to **Pyrford Church** (60m) then cross the road and go up through the graveyard (100m). Pass through the next

field to the far corner (100m). Join the track outside and go R along the field boundaries (550m).

③ Carry on ahead into the last field below the wood (70m) but, in mid-field, just before the pylons turn R across to the edge (100m). Bear L round the protruding corner and go on along the edge and out via the drive to the road at Glebe House (200m). Opposite, take the path beside the drive (200m). At the golf course keep on ahead with the waymarks (300m).

④ The signs then go L along a track (200m). Just before the road turn R around the perimeter of the golf course to the bridge near Pyrford Lock and the ***Anchor*** (200m). Cross the canal. ✳☆

ⓒ *Short cut along the Navigation: Follow the towpath past the lock and on to the next footbridge, Pigeon House Bridge (600m).* ➜⑧

⑤ Continue on the footpath in line with the bridge. Follow this winding path to a tarmac golf track (250m). (**Wisley Church** is visible L and can be reached via the tarmac track then a footbridge L after the R bend).

⑥ Go R along the tarmac track to the clubhouse (400m).

⑦ Near the golf car park fork R (100m) then R again along the gravel track. Follow the waymarks to the towpath at Pigeon House (foot) Bridge (600m). Turn L.

ⓢ *Short cut past the summer-house of* **Pyrford Place**: *Stay on the towpath to Walsham Gates (900m).* ➜⑪ Go on.

⑧ Stay on the towpath briefly (100m) then take the footpath L, over the River Wey and on. At the track continue to **Ockham Mill** (700m), L over the mill tail and on along the lane (150m). ☆

⑨ Turn off R along the winding footpath passing over streams to the wood (400m). After the 2nd bridge, ignore the L fork and keep on to Ripley Green (100m). ✳

⑩ Walk across the grass to the nearest house R (200m) and go down the lane beside it over the millstream to the next house (200m) and straight on along the footpath between the fields to **Walsham Gates** (300m). Cross the sluice gate bridge and go round to the lock keeper's cottage to see the turf lock (100m). Return ⑪ over the sluice bridge (100m) and stay on the tow path (1000m). Cross the Navigation at the lock near Newark Priory. Carry on to the road at Newark Bridge (350m). Cross the bridge to the car park.

The grey stone with glinting quartz grains in old churches around Woking is heathstone from the Chobham and Bagshot heaths. Great blocks of it are unearthed sporadically from the Tertiary (Barton) Sands. Root fossils suggest the blocks were a soil layer perhaps on mud flats when the Sands were beaches 40m years ago. In this rock-deficient region the cut stone has found its way into prestige buildings with brick, flint and puddingstone. Blocks dug by the Basingstoke Canal navvies became coping stones on lock walls and cap stones on the bridges.

Sarsens are blocks of the same stone left on the surface by erosion, even in areas where the Tertiary Sands have entirely disappeared. Stonehenge is mainly sarsens. Churches with sarsens in their foundations may have been sited over pagan temples.

19 Basingstoke Canal meets Wey Navigation

About 7½km/4½ miles with an extension of 2½ km/1½ miles via Byfleet and Wisley Churches. A flat walk along the towpaths, made circular by town roads. Best when spring flowers are in the gardens. OS maps 1:25000 145 Guildford +160 Windsor; 1:50000 176 West London + 186 Aldershot.

Start in Shearwater Road, parking in the wide section near the railway bridge, TQ 037 607, or in one of the side roads. There is parking beside the towpath at Scotland Bridge, TQ 046 615, Old Parvis Road, TQ 055 612, and Murray's Lane, Byfleet, TQ 056 604.

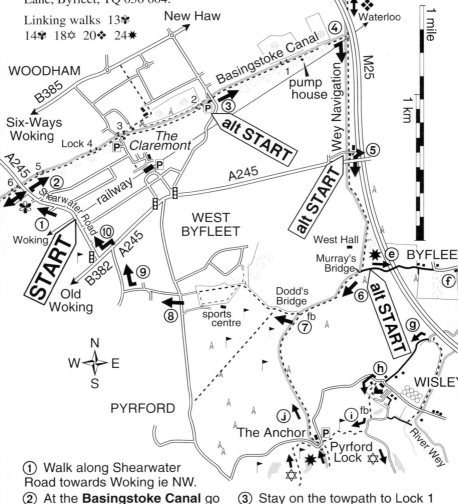

① Walk along Shearwater Road towards Woking ie NW.

② At the **Basingstoke Canal** go R on the towpath from Lock No 6 past Locks, 5, 4, 3 & 2 to the next road at Scotland Bridge (1400m).

③ Stay on the towpath to Lock 1 (550m), the **pump** house (100m) and the **Wey Navigation** junction under the M25 (350m). ❖

38

④ Cross the footbridge and turn R. Follow the towpath under the (**London-Southampton**) railway bridge and on to the next road bridges (800m).

⑤ Ascend to the road, skirt round the works yard and carry on along the towpath to Murray's (cart) Bridge at **Byfleet** (850m). ✳

ⓔ *Extension of 2½ km/1½ miles: Go L on the track from the bridge, over the M25 and ahead on the road to* **Byfleet Church** *(750m).*

ⓕ *Enter the churchyard and follow the footpath parallel with Sanway Road, out to the road junction (250m). From the road bend carry on along the narrow road ahead then the hard track and pass under the M25 (350m).*

ⓖ *When the hard track enters an enclosure, take the track R beside the fence to* **Wisley** *(400m).*

ⓗ *At the road go R a few steps (50m) and enter the churchyard L. Pass round the church and follow the path through the golf course, over the footbridge to the tarmac drive (300m).*

ⓘ *Go R on the drive (100m) then turn off at the bend along the winding footpath to the Wey Navigation at Pyrford Lock and the* **Anchor** *(250m).*

ⓙ *Go past the pub, along the towpath, to the 1st footbridge over the Navigation (900m).* ➜⑦

⑥ Keep on beside the Navigation to the next footbridge (900m). ✡

⑦ Cross the Navigation and follow the boundary path ahead or the lesser path parallel with it at the edge of the golf course. After the golf course (500m) keep on through the field and out between houses to the road (400m).

⑧ Cross and follow the Holybank Road, opposite, to the end (400m).

⑨ Go R to the main road in West Byfleet (300m).

⑩ Turn L (100m) then R along Shearwater Road to the start.

SUSSEX was one of the locomotives that pulled the first regular trains to Woking in 1838. The London & South West Railway Company bought twelve similar engines @ £1,650 each from Tayleurs of Newton-le-Willows in Lancashire. With only single drive wheels and 8 tons weight they were soon superseded. Presumably they were delivered by barge.

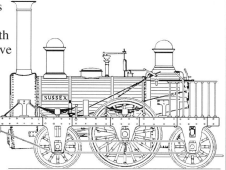

L&SWR Locomotives 1838-53 D L Bradley 1965 265pp © Wild Swan Publications

The **London - Southampton** main line of the L&SWR was one of the earliest railways to open for long distance public traffic, being preceded only by the Manchester to Liverpool Railway in 1830 and the South Carolina Railroad in 1831. The first public train ran to Woking Common Station on 21st May 1838 - a week before the first public train of the GWR to Maidenhead and a month before the Manchester-Birmingham railway was completed. The Southampton and London halves were linked in 1839 and the London terminus moved from Nine Elms to Waterloo in 1848. The line was widened to 4 tracks in 1903.

20 The Navigation, Coxes Lock and Wey Bridge

A flat 5½ km/3½ miles; along the Wey Navigation and River Wey, with linear extensions of 3½ km/2 miles to the River Thames and 2½ km/1½ miles to the the Basingstoke Canal junction; surprisingly shady and tranquil.
OS maps 1:25000 60 Windsor; 1:50000 176 West London.

Start from the car park at New Haw Lock, TQ 055 630. On the extension, start from the riverside car park, TQ 075 657.

Linking walks 57❖ 50★ 51❄

The White Hart ☎ 01932 842927
The Old Crown ☎ 01932 842844
The Minnow ☎ 01932 831672
Thames Court ☎ 01932 221957
Nauticalia Ferry 01932 254844

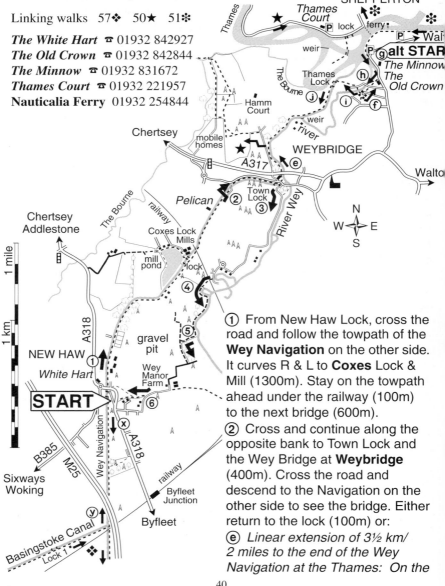

① From New Haw Lock, cross the road and follow the towpath of the **Wey Navigation** on the other side. It curves R & L to **Coxes** Lock & Mill (1300m). Stay on the towpath ahead under the railway (100m) to the next bridge (600m).

② Cross and continue along the opposite bank to Town Lock and the Wey Bridge at **Weybridge** (400m). Cross the road and descend to the Navigation on the other side to see the bridge. Either return to the lock (100m) or:

ⓔ *Linear extension of 3½ km/ 2 miles to the end of the Wey Navigation at the Thames: On the*

40

opposite side of the road from the lock take the path down to the river bank and continue ahead on the towpath under the next road bridge. Note for future use the little footbridge L just before the R curve (300m). ★ *Stay on the towpath past the weir where river & canal split (400m) to* **Thames Lock** *(400m). Look for the 3rd lock gate downstream. Cross the footbridge and keep on over the tarmac drive (150m) and the River Wey footbridge (50m).*

(f) *At the little road go L to the bend and ahead on the footpath between houses. Cross another road and keep on to the main road at the* **Old Crown** *(200m). Walk down the road to the River Thames (200m), through the car park and on along the river bank to the bend (150m).* ✤
If you cross the Thames walk L to Shepperton Lock & **Thames Court**. *Return by the same route to the old Wey bridge.*

(g) *For people starting from the Thames-side car park: Follow the road away from the Thames past the* **Minnow** *(100m) and on to the* **Old Crown** *(100m).*

(h) *Turn R between the pub and its car park and follow the footpath between houses, over a road and ahead (200m).*

(i) *Just into the next little road turn R over the River Wey foot-bridge and the tarmac drive (50m). Continue ½L on the footpath to* **Thames Lock** *(150m).*

(j) *Cross the footbridge and go L along the Wey Navigation past the 2nd weir L where it rejoins the river (400m), round the twist in the*

river at the house (100m), under the modern road bridge and up onto the old Wey Bridge in Weybridge (300m). ➔③

③ Follow the little road down round the end of the lock (250m) and carry on beside the river then round several bends to the mobile home estate (850m). Take the road along the boundary L to the 4-way junction (80m).

④ Start along the curving road L (50m) then cross the railway R. Follow the footpath across the narrow field ahead (70m). In the next field follow the track round L to the River **Wey** (120m). Carry on beside it (300m). Eventually the track bends away from the river to a T-junction (150m).

⑤ Go L (200m). At the next T-junction turn R and follow the track round a L bend (100m) then a R bend and L to the farm house (100m). Join the tarmac drive and follow it round the R bend (50m) and on to the houses R (200m).

⑥ Just before the houses take the footpath R round the end of the field and join the road near the bridge over the Navigation at New Haw Lock (250m). The **White Hart** is just over the bridge.

(x) *Linear extension of 2½ km/1½ miles to the* **Basingstoke Canal**: *From New Haw Lock follow the* **Wey Navigation** *towpath away from the road all the way to the M25 bridge (1000m) and under it to the branching Basingstoke Canal and the* **London-Southampton** *railway bridge (200m).* ❖ *Return.*

(y) *Follow the towpath under the M25 to New Haw Lock (1200m).*

21 Thorpe Green and St Ann's Hill

About 7 km/4¼ miles extending by 2½km/1½ miles to Thorpe village; over fields and wood with quite a lot of road walking; undulating; brambles and nettles in summer. OS maps 1:25000 160 Windsor; 1:50000 176 West London.

Start at Thorpe Green car park, TQ 010 679, or a roadside parking place on St Ann's Hill, TQ 028 67.

Rose and Crown ☎ 01322 845154
The Golden Grove ☎ 01932 562132
The Red Lion ☎ 01932 563350

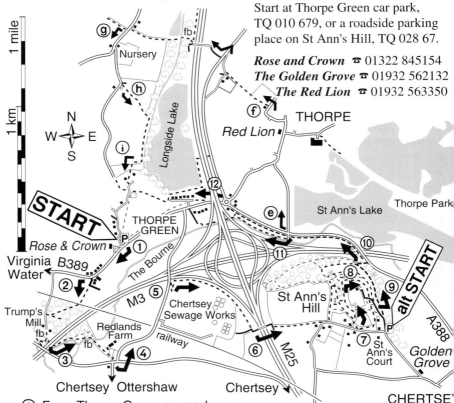

① From Thorpe Green car park cross to the ***Rose & Crown*** and go on along the road (300m).

② On the R bend, after the last house, go L on the track to the field (40m) and down the R edge (150m). Cross the railway lines and bear R along the path through the wood (150m) then R to the tarmac drive (50m). Walk down the drive (L) past **Trump's Mill** R and cottage L (100m) and on along the footpath (50m).

③ Don't cross the Bourne bridge but drop L and cross the mill tail.

Stay beside the **Bourne** under the road (400m). At the end of the wood cross the footbridge and go up the R edge of the field past **Redlands Farm**, across a narrow field and R to the road (150m).

④ Turn L and L again and walk up Lyne Lane over the railway and on to the motorway bridge (700m).

⑤ Just before the bridge take the path R down the embankment and follow the edge of the road up beside Chertsey Sewage Works to the farm bridge (750m).

⑥ Cross the M25 (150m). Slightly R take the footpath between the fields (300m) and continue up the lane ahead. Ignore the path up L (50m) and carry on to the next path L (150m), after The Lodge.

⑦ Turn L for **St Ann's Hill**. Inside go L to the hedge near The Lodge (70m) and ascend beside it. When the hedge bends L (30m) continue up, disregarding all side paths, to the beacon on top (300m).

⑧ Just before the beacon turn R on the path which curves around the brow of the hill (200m). When the track crosses from the garden, turn L down it. Ignore the 1st side track L (50m) and continue to the track rising from below (100m).

⑨ Turn back L down this track (Old Coach Road)(400m).

⑩ Near the bottom, watch out for the path R and go down it to the road (Mill House Lane) (80m). Turn L and walk along the horse ride verge over the M3 (200m) and the Bourne (250m). Carry on to Mill Lane (200m).

ⓔ *Extension to **Thorpe** village mainly on roads: Walk along Mill Lane past fields (500m) then R on the road through the village to the **Red Lion** (200m). Go on round L & R bends to the 1st field (300m).*

ⓕ *Take the footpath L to the end (400m) and go R along the lane to the road (200m). A little L (30m) join the track on the other side and go over the motorway (200m). After the bridge take the footpath R down into the trees, over the footbridge and along the edge of the field to the next road (400m).*

ⓖ *Walk L along the pavement (100m) and L along the 1st side*

lane to the R bend (250m).

ⓗ *Take the footpath L between drives. The path bends R (300m) and carries on under trees (300m).*

ⓘ *At the field go R briefly (30m) then L and between houses to the green in Thorpe Green (150m). Go straight over the grass near the R edge to the car park (400m).*

⑪ Opposite Mill Lane turn L to the river (50m). Go R along the bank (350m) and rejoin the road (100m).

⑫ Keep on to the roundabout and under the M25 (250m). Just out the other side take the path R through the trees to the green in Thorpe Green (100m) and make your way, parallel with the road, to the car park at the end (500m). The tower visible far R was part of Holloway Sanatorium.

St Ann's Hill, the most easterly hump of the Bagshot Sands, is a landmark for the adjacent M25/M3 junction. It was part of the grounds of St Ann's Court, home of the statesman Charles Fox who acquired it by marrying his mistress, Mrs Armistead. The Prince Regent (later George IV) came here to moon over Mrs Fitzherbert but fell out with Fox when he married her. The name is from a medieval chapel on the hill. The Iron Age hill fort on top provided the old name, Aldbury. The Dingle, near the road, was a sandpit until the 20th century.

Trump's Mill is on a site dating to before 1299. It paid tithes of 21s 4d to Chertsey Abbey. The water is from the Bourne. The footbridges cross the mill tail. Milling ceased in 1909.

Redlands Farm is a hall house of about 1490. The chimney and second storey would have been inserted in the next 50 years when the jutting new wing was added.

22 Chertsey Bridge to Shepperton Ferry

About 7 km/4½ miles with short extensions; flat; over meadows and along the Thames Path with a ferry crossing. The ferry operates 8-6 weekdays, 9-6 Saturdays and 10-6 Sundays; but only until 5pm on winter weekends. OS maps 1:25000 160 Windsor; 1:50000 176 West London.

Start from Mead Lane car park in Chertsey next to the marina, TQ 054 662, or the public car park TQ 071 659, next to *The Thames Court* at Shepperton Lock, or the car park near the ferry in Weybridge, TQ 075 657. At the east end of Chertsey bridge there is a minute car park and a larger one 100m further E.

Linking walks   20★   23☆   **Nauticalia Ferry** ☎ 01932 254844
The Old Crown ☎ 01932 842844   *The Minnow* ☎ 01932 831672
The Kingfisher ☎ 01932 579811   *Thames Court* ☎ 01932 221957

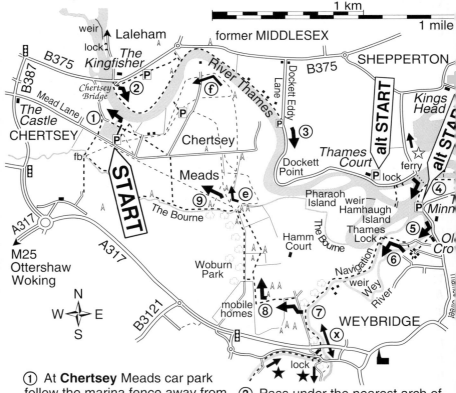

① At **Chertsey** Meads car park follow the marina fence away from the road (100m) and turn L along the footpath over the marina channel (100m). Carry straight on along the track and road to the main road (300m)(see **Curfew Bell** effigy L).

② Pass under the nearest arch of **Chertsey Bridge** then cross the river (150m). See Chertsey Lock upstream L. At the Middlesex end cross the main road or go under the bridge again. Opposite *the Kingfisher* follow the Thames

44

Path along the river bank (1600m) or the path near the road across the 1st meander (300m less).

③ At the road carry on ahead on the grassy path beside the tarmac round Dockett Point and past the boats of Pharoah Island dwellers, the **Thames Court** (1000m) and **Shepperton Lock** (200m) to the bend in the road (100m). ☆ Cross the river on the **Nauticalia** ferry.

④ From the ferry landing follow the path round the curving river

---

View of the river: Facing the weir the narrow channel L is the mouth of the River Wey and the site of the wharf. The next channel is the start of the Wey Navigation and the 3rd is the original bed of the Thames sweeping round an elongated meander from the weir opposite *The Thames Court*. Out of sight the Bourne joins the meander in the middle. The 4th channel with the weir used by canoeists, is Stoner Gut, an artificial channel which detaches Hamhaugh Island within the meander. The 5th channel is the cut for Shepperton Lock. Downstream of the ferry is D'Oyly Carte Island where lived the theatrical family.

---

bank to the car park (150m). Take the road ahead past the **Minnow** (100m) and on (100m).

⑤ Turn R between the **Old Crown** and its car park and follow the footpath between gardens, over the 1st road and ahead on the next path (200m).

⑥ At the little road don't continue on the footpath but turn R over the River **Wey** footbridge then the tarmac drive (50m). Continue ½L on the footpath to **Thames Lock** (150m). Notice the 3rd lockgate downstream. Cross the bridge and

go L along the **Wey Navigation** past the 2nd weir L where the river separates (400m), round the twist in the river at the house (100m) and on round the next L curve. Watch out for a little footbridge over the ditch back R (300m).

ⓧ *Extension: Continue on the tow path under the modern road bridge to the old Wey bridge in* **Weybridge** *(300m). ★*
Go out onto this bridge then back along the tow path (300m). ➔⑧

⑦ Cross the little footbridge to the road and go R to the gate of Hamm Court Farm (100m). Take the path L and cross the field to the mobile home estate (300m).

⑧ Go R along the boundary to the corner of the estate (200m) then either straight on over the fields between the pylons, ultimately exiting at the far L corner (500m) or L along the end of the estate and R down the path outside the field. Exit to the cart bridge and cross the **Bourne** to Chertsey Meads.

ⓔ *Extension: From the bridge go briefly L (20m) then take one of the paths directly away from the Bourne to the lane (400m). Cross and go straight on over the meads to the bank of the Thames (600m).*

ⓕ *Turn L and follow paths beside the river and round the houses to the car park at the marina (700m).*

⑨ From the bridge identify St Ann's Hill ½L on the horizon and aim directly for it over the meads diverging from the Bourne; there is usually a faint path (700m). When Mead Lane converges R keep on near it to the car park near the marina (200m).

23 Walton Bridge and Shepperton

About 6½ km/4 miles but variable; along the Thames Path and on the lanes through Old Shepperton; flat. It involves a ferry crossing. The Nauticalia Ferry operates 8-6 weekdays, 9-6 Saturdays and 10-6 Sundays but only until 5pm in winter. OS maps: 1:25000 160 Windsor; 1:50000 176 West London.

Start from Walton Bridge car park, TQ 092 663, or the public car park beside the *Thames Court* near Shepperton Lock, TQ 071 659, or the car park near the ferry in Weybridge, TQ 075 657, or the recreation ground car park in Church Road, Shepperton, TQ 078 668.

Linking walk 20❋ 22☆

Nauticalia Ferry ☎ 01932 254844
The Minnow ☎ 01932 831672
The Kings Head ☎ 01932 221910
The Red Lion ☎ 01932 220042
The Old Crown ☎ 01932 842844
The Thames Court ☎ 01932 221957
The Ship Hotel ☎ 01932 227320

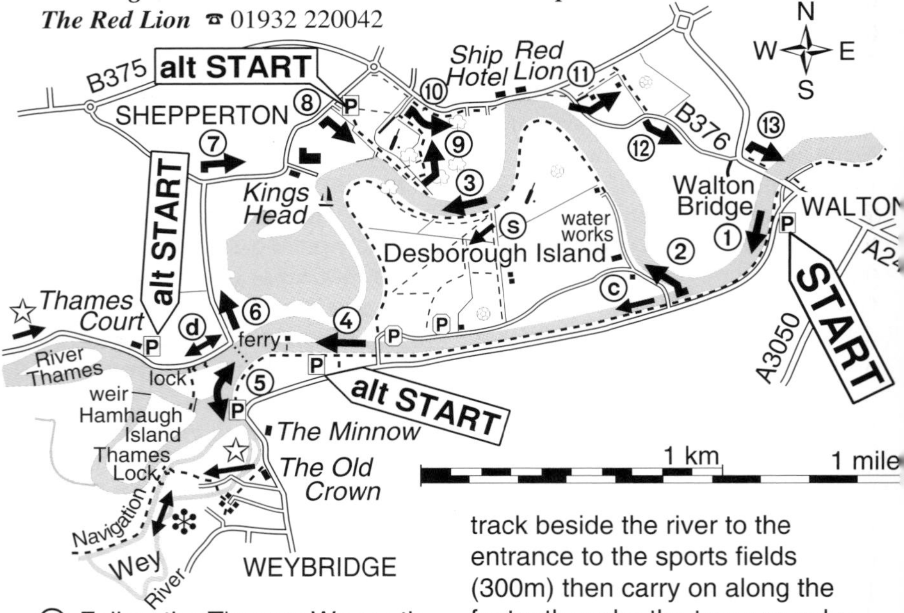

① Follow the Thames Way path on the river bank upstream away from **Walton** Bridge, past **Cowey Stakes**, to the next bridge (500m).

Ⓒ *Short cut saving 1 km/¾ mile: Carry on ahead beside the* ***Desborough*** *Cut to the next road bridge (1000m).* ➔④

② Ascend to the bridge and cross to Desborough Island. (200m). When the road bends L take the track beside the river to the entrance to the sports fields (300m) then carry on along the footpath under the trees round a bend in the river until paths branch L into the fields (700m).

Ⓢ *Short cut: Turn away from the river and follow the diagonal path through the fields, to the next bridge (600m). Over the bridge the route is R along the river.* ➔④

③ In the field take the path near the river (300m) then continue under the trees on the bank again opposite Shepperton Church and Manor House (600m) back to the road. Cross the bridge and drop to the river bank (100m). Turn R.

④ Continue along the Thames (upstream) past the footbridge of D'Oyly Carte Island (300m) and on round the curve. Watch out for the ferry quay (100m). ☆

⑤ Keep on round the curve in the river to the little car park (150m). ❊ (the *Minnow* and *Old Crown* are a little further along the road) then return along the river bank and cross to **Shepperton** via the ferry.

ⓓ *Detour: Follow the road beside the river to see **Shepperton Lock** (100m) (the pub **Thames Court** is a little further on (200m)) then return to the bend in the lane at the ferry jetty.*

⑥ Follow Ferry Lane away from the river to the end (600m).

⑦ Turn R along Chertsey Road to **Shepperton** village centre (300m). After the *Kings Head* and the church carry on out of the old village (300m).

⑧ At the recreation ground car park turn R and follow the path along the edge of the field and on to the end of the wall R (200m) then join the river bank and continue (100m).

⑨ Turn L over the riverside path in the trees and go on along the winding path outside the cricket field (250m). Follow the drive towards the road (100m).

⑩ Just before the road turn R on the footpath. Follow it until it joins the road at the *Ship*. Keep on beside the road past the *Red Lion* (300m) almost to the next R, Walton Lane (100m).

⑪ Cut across the corner R and across Walton Lane and go on over the grass next to the frontages (200m). Turn R round the corner in the wall and follow the path beside the football field out to re-join Walton Lane (200m).

⑫ Turn L and follow the lane to the end (400m).

⑬ Cross the road and cross Walton Bridge (200m) and take the steps down L. Go under the bridge, back to the car park.

The **Thames** is an ancient highway for traffic. A 2nd century barge exposed during building work at Barts Hospital was 15m long but there may have been larger ones; a Dutch boat of the same age was 34m long. Barges were swim-headed (punt shaped) until superseded by Newbury barges (pointed) in the 18th century. They had sails which could be deployed when the wind was in the right direction. Tow ropes were attached at the masthead. Until the 18th century the towing was done by local squads of men called *halers*.

Locks are only needed because of the weirs. The weirs are needed to make the water deep enough for navigation. The earliest weirs were probably built to provide a head of water for mills so the Thames might be viewed as a series of mill ponds or pounds. The first pound locks (ie with two sets of gates) were installed on the Thames in 1760. They permit a weir to control the upstream level - still the main job of the lock keeper. Before that there were flashlocks. These were gaps in weirs that could be opened to let boats through (with great difficulty and hazard) and cause a flash of water to raise the level down-river.

The Thames Highway II Fred Thacker 1920 & 1968 David & Charles 525pp
The Thames from source to tideway P H Chaplin 1982 Whittet Books 192pp

24 Pyrford Lock, Byfleet and Wisley

About 8 km/5 miles; flat; a Wey Navigation walk but near the M25 and through a housing estate to make the route circular. OS 1:25000 145 Guildford +160 Windsor; 1:50000 187 Dorking.

Start from Pyrford Lock, TQ 053 593, or Wisley Common car park, TQ 065 589, or in Murray's Lane near Byfleet old church, TQ 060 604.

Linking walks 53✧ 55☆ 56✳ 57✶ 59✦

The Anchor ☎ 01932 342507

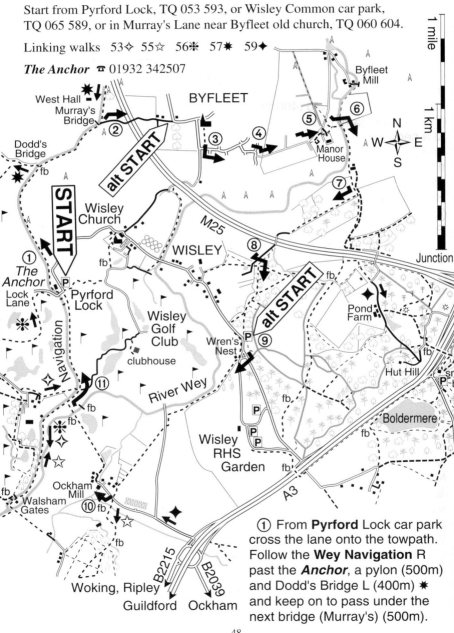

① From **Pyrford** Lock car park cross the lane onto the towpath. Follow the **Wey Navigation** R past the *Anchor*, a pylon (500m) and Dodd's Bridge L (400m) ✶ and keep on to pass under the next bridge (Murray's) (500m).

② Join the track from the bridge and pass over the motorway. Keep on ahead to **Byfleet Church** (750m). Follow the path along the middle of the churchyard to the road junction behind (250m).

③ On the road go L (300m) and take the 3rd R (150m).

④ Round the R bend in Fullerton Road turn L on the concrete farm track between the houses and follow it across the field (400m).

⑤ When the farm track bends R at a hedge, go through the hedge and ahead past stables (100m). At the drive go L to the side path R after the gates of **Byfleet Manor House** (70m).

⑥ Follow the footpath over the River **Wey** (100m) then R beside it to Park Barn Farm (300m) and on (250m). ✦

⑦ Enter the end of the 1st field R and go down the L edge, through a belt of trees and on to the corner (100m). Join the track over the M25 (100m). Don't take the side path down the bank but keep to the track beside the wood (300m).

⑧ Just after a ditch and boundary, turn L into the wood. Almost immediately (30m) turn R on the woodland path. Stay on this path, near the edge of the wood, to Wisley Common (Wren's Nest) car park (500m).

⑨ From the car park cross the road and follow the pavement L (100m) then take the footpath at Wren's Nest cottage between fences through **Wisley Garden** to the next lane (800m). Cross and continue diagonally over the fields. After the houses skirt round a garden to Mill Lane (600m). ☆

⑩ Turn R and go along the lane to **Ockham Mill** (100m). Cross the mill tail and carry on along the track past the houses, out through a gateway (200m). Continue on the footpath and cross the River Wey to the towpath of the Navigation (450m). ❋◇

⑪ Go R on the towpath, passing Pigeon House (foot) Bridge L and a footpath into Wisley Golf Course R (100m). Carry on to Pyrford Lock (600m) and the car park.

Locks with pairs of gates are pound locks. The earliest known were on the Peking Grand Canal before 1300. By the next century they were in use in Holland. The first recorded in Britain were installed at Exeter around 1567. Experience with locks to adapt rivers as Navigations made possible the true canals. The first to be independent of a river in England was built in 1761 by the Duke of Bridgewater to convey coal from his mines to Manchester.

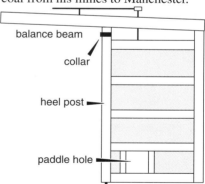

The timber gate of a small canal lock has a great *balance beam* increasing the operator's leverage but decreasing the sideways strain on the top hinge - usually a simple iron collar round the *heel post*. The iron heel at the bottom rotates in an iron socket set in the sill. The sluice for filling and emptying the lock, the *paddle gear,* is incorporated in the gate or built into the lock wall.

25 Wisley Common and Airfield

About 9½ km/6 miles or 1 km/¾ mile extra via *The Hautboy* in Ockham;
heath, woods and farmland. Wisley Common is boggy in winter but pools can
be skirted. OS maps: 1:25000 new 145 Guildford; 1:50000 187 Dorking

Start from the Wren's Nest car park on Wisley Lane, TQ 065 589, or from
Commons Car Park near the A3/M25 slip road on Old Lane, TQ 078 586.

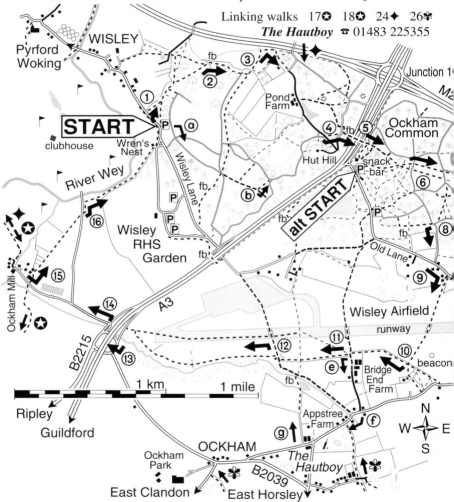

Linking walks 17✪ 18✪ 24✦ 26❀
The Hautboy ☎ 01483 225355

① Leave Wisley Common car
park on the footpath diverging
from the road northwards (away
from Wren's Nest)(300m). Fork R
near a field corner and keep on to
the edge of the Common (250m).

② Follow the boundary R, past
the end of a wide track to a cross
path (300m) and turn L over the
bridge towards the M25 (200m).
③ Near the motorway turn R
towards the hillock (100m) and

50

skirt round it to the hard track (200m). Keep on down the hard track past Pond Farm and the pond, to Hut Hill R, watching out for the path L opposite the 2nd exit from the track R (550m).

④ Follow the path to the old car park (150m) and go straight on over the A3 footbridge (250m). (The path R skirting the hillock leads to the snack bar (200m) and Commons Car Park).

⑤ Keep to the path ahead L of the hillock, ignoring numerous side paths to a wide oblique cross path (300m) then fork L to the wide **heath** track (100m).

⑥ Continue on the path ahead ever upwards to Chatley **Semaphore Tower** (700m). ❀

⑦ Walk down the clearing below the tower (100m) and join the downhill horse track under the trees L. Descend past side tracks L (200m) & R (150m) to the wide cross track (200m).

⑧ Go L to the road (300m).

⑨ Walk along the road L (150m). On the L curve, next to a drive take the path R (60m). In the field continue along the hedge (100m). When it bends L go straight on and over the runway of the disused **Wisley Airfield** to the boundary fence (600m) after the circular air navigation **beacon** L.

⑩ Over the fence turn R along the path to the farm track (400m).

ⓔ *Extension to the **Hautboy**: Go L through the farm and down to the road in **Ockham** (400m).*

ⓕ *Walk R along the pavement or, after 100m, along the edge of the cricket field to the hotel (450m).*

ⓖ *After the barns opposite the hotel take the drive L up to the fields (250m). Continue on the footpath at the R edge of the field (200m) then ½L past the pond in the little valley (150m). After the footbridge go L up the track (200m).* ➛⑫

⑪ Continue on the boundary path (500m) and drop to the track.

⑫ Ascend over the brow of the hill to the runway (200m). Stay on it to the L end then drop to the A3 slip road (950m).

⑬ Walk L to the roundabout, under the A3 and back on the slip road R on the other side (300m).

⑭ Turn L and stay on Mill Lane to **Ockham Mill** (700m). ❂➛

⑮ Return along the lane (150m) and take the footpath, now L, up past the houses and across the fields to the golfclub drive (600m).

⑯ Cross and take the footpath briefly L near the road then R to the River **Wey**, along the bank and on past the **Wisley Garden** to Wren's Nest cottage (800m). Walk along the pavement L to the car park (100m).

ⓐ Another time, start on the soft track beyond the car park and go R (200m). Cross a track from the road and carry on to a 6-way junction of tracks (400m). Still continue ahead (300m).

ⓑ Take the 2nd side path L up over the little rise to a junction (100m) and keep on ahead on the broad winding soft track which eventually passes around the foot of Hut Hill (700m). At the end cross the hard track. ➛④

26 Ockham and Chatley Semaphore Tower

About 6½ km/4 miles or 10½ km/6½ miles.
Farmland, wood and heath. OS maps: 1:25000
145 Guildford; 1:50000 187 Dorking.

Start at Pond Car Park, TQ 079 583, off the
M25/A3 junction slip road on Old Lane .

Linking walk 25✿

The Black Swan ☎ 01932 862364
The Hautboy ☎ 01483 225355

Wisley Pyrford Woking

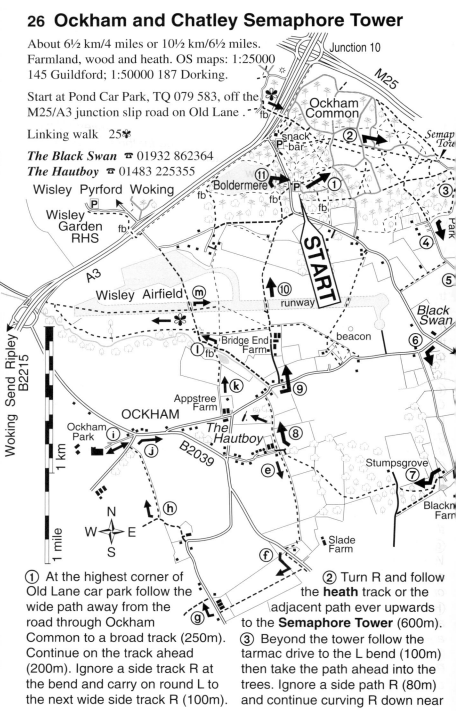

① At the highest corner of
Old Lane car park follow the
wide path away from the
road through Ockham
Common to a broad track (250m).
Continue on the track ahead
(200m). Ignore a side track R at
the bend and carry on round L to
the next wide side track R (100m).

② Turn R and follow
the **heath** track or the
adjacent path ever upwards
to the **Semaphore Tower** (600m).
③ Beyond the tower follow the
tarmac drive to the L bend (100m)
then take the path ahead into the
trees. Ignore a side path R (80m)
and continue curving R down near

52

the edge of the wood beside Hatchford Park, round a R bend at the Samuelson monument (300m) and down to the houses (150m).

④ Go L on the drive L all the way to the road (550m).

⑤ Follow the road R round bends L & R to the **Black Swan** (550m).

⑥ After the crossroads stay on Ockham Lane briefly (100m) then turn off L on the farm drive. Follow it through the fields and round the R bend at the house (900m).

⑦ When the drive bends L go over the bridge and ½L into the wood (100m) then R on the side path to the far corner of the wood (250m). Slightly R (30m) take the track on the other side through the next wood (350m). In the field at the end, cross ½R to the middle of the bottom edge; in the next, to the far R corner. Go out to the track junction near the house (550m).

ⓔ *Extended version via Ockham Church: Go L along the edge of the fields (700m). In the last field go R past the house and through the trees to the road (100m).*

ⓕ *Cross slightly L (20m) follow the roadside bridleway (150m). Just after Slade Farm drive turn R and keep on between fields up to the next road (600m).*

ⓖ *Walk along the road R (550m). When it bends R take the track ahead past the buildings and carry on between fields (250m).*

ⓗ *At the L bend, take the path ahead to the next road (550m) and go R to the T-junction (100m).*

ⓘ *If you wish to see **Ockham Park** and church and quietly contemplate **Occam's Razor**, go up the drive L then return (200m).*

ⓙ *Follow the road, R, through Ockham (250m). Fork L at the war memorial to the **Hautboy** (400m).*

ⓚ *Opposite the hotel go up the drive L of the barns to the fields (250m) then take the path at the R edge of the field (200m) & ½L past the pond in the little valley (150m).*

ⓛ *Over the footbridge, go up the track L . Stay ahead to the runway in the top field (350m).* ✿

ⓜ *Walk along the runway R to the track crossing from the next farm R (500m). Turn L.* ➔⑩

⑧ Go R beside the farm. At the sports field stay outside the trees to the road in **Ockham** (400m). (The **Hautboy** is L across the sports field. ➔ⓚ)

⑨ Go R on the road (150m). Don't turn on the track L after the bridge but up the drive after Bridge End House. Continue ahead through the farm and over the field to **Wisley Airfield** runway (500m). ✿

⑩ Go on along the horse track and the house drive (600m). At the track junction don't turn to the road but carry on into the wood (150m).

⑪ After the bridge pass between the trees L to Boldermere (100m) then R to the car park (150m).

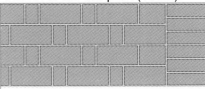

Rat trap bond is the pattern of bricks laid on edge. It was favoured on the Ockham estate in the Victorian period and can be seen - usually relieved by decorative brickwork - in some of the houses and barns, and *The Hautboy*. Three flat bricks match two on edge in door and window surrounds.

Anthony's is the cluster of houses at the NE corner of Horsell Common. There used to be five Chertsey almshouses there and, around 1850 an Anthony Ives lived in one of them. Perhaps people went to Anthony's.

The **Basingstoke Canal** is 37 miles long. It started from the Wey Navigation at Byfleet in 1796 at the apogee of the canal building period. Not linking areas of industry and dense population it was perceived as the first agricultural canal - food to London; coal and horse dung to the country but it did not pay for itself. The peak year for traffic was 1838 when the railway was built. The last barge tied up at Basingstoke in 1910. The canal is now owned by Surrey and Hants County Councils. Cut by the M3 it is navigable only to Odiham Castle.
                      London's Lost Route to Basingstoke P A L Vine 1968 David & Charles 212pp

The **Beacon** on Wisley Airfield is a VHF Omnidirectional Rangefinder, VOR. An aircraft detects its exact position from it without reference to any other beacon. There are about 50 such beacons in Britain and the chief aircraft lanes cross them. This VOR is also the centre for one of Heathrow's four stacking circuits (the others are at Biggin Hill, Bovington & Lambourne).

Barrows are burial mounds. About 100 are known in Surrey, mostly Bonze Age; many have disappeared through gravel extraction, ploughing etc. The Horsell Common bell barrow, dated 1400-1200 BC, still has its ditch.
            Surrey Barrows 1934-1986, a reappraisal Lesleie Grinstead SAC vol 78 1987 41pp

The **Bee Gardens** on Chobham Common are ancient earthworks of unknown age and use. They may have been convenient markers for positioning hives in summer, but it is unlikely they were constructed for this. The smaller, near the east boundary, appears to be a moated enclosure and probably held a house. The larger encloses about 2 acres and might have been a corral for livestock.

Bisley was listed as part of Chobham in a Chertsey Abbey charter of 933. The name was spelt *Busselegh* which may derive from 'bushy clearing'. The tenant of 1284 held the estate as a parcel of Byfleet and was patron of its church. The little church, St John the Baptist, has nave walls of puddingstone and heath stone which probably date from about that time. Bisley is known throughout the world for shooting. Besides hosting national and international competitions it is home to about 30 shooting clubs for a wide range of small arms. The NFA National Rifle Association was formed in 1860 having roots in the Volunteers. It was pushed out of Wimbledon Common by the growth of London and acquired Bisley Common in 1890. The army paid and have retained the ranges ever since but the clubs have their own buildings . The NFA has a museum open two days a week (☎ 01483-797777). In the early days the NRA had its own railway - the bridge pillars still stand near Lock 15.

The **Bourne** starts as trickles on Bagshot Heath and Chobham Ridges which become the Windle Brook then the Millbourne of Chobham. It joins the main Bourne near Fairoaks, collects the outflow from Virginia Water and flows beside Chertsey Meads to the Thames. The word is the same as *burn*.

Brick Hill is a disorganised hamlet of mainly small houses originally for the workers at nearby claypits. The earliest evidence of brickmaking here appears in 1751 and by 1860, when Woking was rapidly expanding, six companies were at work. The clay is part of the Bagshot Sands.

Broadmead was the medieval common pasture of 365 acres with about 50 owners in the 19th century. It was open for grazing by the commoners of Send and Woking from September 18th to March, the rest of year being for hay.

Brook Place, the finest Dutch-style house in the area, is an ecumenical conference centre and retreat. The house was built in 1656 by William Beauchamp. The previous house belonged to Edward Bray who was awarded the property by Charles I for raising a troup of horse. In Chertsey Abbey's manorial records for Chobham a William de Broke was deprived of his tenancy for poor farming in 1302.

Brookwood is a narrow strip between the Basingstoke Canal and the railway which grew at the extremity of Woking parish because of the cemetery. The station was interpolated in 1864 at the junction of the cemetery's private line.

Byfleet was a small village which expanded towards Woking and became part of the borough in 1933 at the same time as Pyrford. In the Domesday Book it was BIFLET with a church, a mill and fishery taxed @ 325 eels. Edward II acquired it from the abbey in circumstances unknown and gave it to Piers Gaveston. Later it was property of the Black Prince and documents signed here show he visited, probably to hunt in the forest. West Byfleet took its name from the station; there is no East Byfleet

Byfleet, a village of England L R Stevens ed 2 1972 Livrevin 110pp

Byfleet Church, St Mary's, is the medieval church with a Victorian church tacked on. It is not close to the old village. The old part may be on the site of the Domesday Book church but was built around 1300. Points of interest: the roofs; brass of Thomas Teylar, Rector 1454-1489, stones in the old walls.

Byfleet Manor House was built in the 1620s for Anne of Denmark, Queen to James I, and the gate pillars date from that time. It has been rebuilt several times but is still a Jacobean mansion.

Chertsey is in Runnymede Borough with Virginia Water, Englefield Green, Egham, Thorpe, Addlestone and Ottershaw. Like many places on the Thames the **y** is derived from the Saxon for island. It was not on any arterial road until the M25 came past but the river would have connected it with the ancient world better than any road. The abbey was founded in 666, destroyed by the Vikings and restarted, ending only with the Dissolution in 1537 (see box p 3). Bede wrote in 731 of the founding of the abbey and explained CERATÆSEI meant Cerot's Island. It was CERTSEY in the Domesday Book.

The Ecclesiastical History of the English People Bede Penguin 1990

Chertsey Bridge is an elegant Georgian link between the town and Middlesex though Pevsner thinks the arches do not fit well with the triangular profile. It was built a few yards upsteam of the old timber bridge in 1785. The earliest known bridge was licensed in 1410 by Henry IV. Sibille the ferrywomen was paid 3s in for transporting the king and family in 1299. Dickens has Oliver Twist crossing it with Sykes on his way to be initiated as a burglar.

Chobham was Chebeham one of the earliest places known from the charter of 673 (see box p3). It was probably the home of a Saxon called Ceabba which is the diminutive of Cædbæd In the Domesday book it was CEBEHÁ, listed as having a church. Henry VIII took the manor for himself at the dissolution of the abbey in 1537. The demesne was imparked around 1558 and became Chobham Park. Queen Mary sold that to Nicholas Heath, Archbishop of York. Although he proclaimed Queen Elizabeth (1558) he refused to crown her and spent the next decade in the Tower for denying church decrees. Later lords of the manor have been the Mores of Loseley, the Zouches of Bramshill and the Onslows of Clandon. *The History of Chobham* Robert Schueller 1989 Phillimore 203pp

Chobham Church, St Lawrence, stands on a Saxon site. Papal licence to bury the dead was granted in 1215; Chertsey Abbey's compensation for loss of trade was 20s and 6 lbs of beeswax p.a. Features of interest: the Norman chalk pillars of the south aisle with fluted capitals of around 1150, the tops of the earlier windows of about 1080 above them and the elbow beams; the chest of around 1250; the 16th century wooden font; the tower of around 1400; north aisle and pillars of 1886; the 1950 memorial screen for two World Wars at the entrance; a plaque about Archbishop Heath near the chancel arch and his burial place, the blue marble stone before the altar.

Chobham Common, presently 1445 acres, was bought by Surrey CC in 1986 @ £1 per acre. Most of it is heath, a consequence of the underlying Tertiary (Bagshot) Sands and Ice Age gravels. Marsh gentian and sundew grow in some of the marshy places and Deptford pinks on high parts. *Sphagnum* moss was harvested in WWI as a wound dressing like cottonwool. Parts of Sunningdale were built on it as was the tank factory that became the army vehicle research centre and test track. Chobham Common, like other Surrey heaths, has been used for army training camps. The 1853 camp was the last before the army went into permanent camp on the heath at Aldershot. The *London Illustrated News* reported 8129 men, 1508 horses and 24 guns took part. *Punch* poked fun. Queen Victoria reviewed the troops as written in stone near Monument car park. The allotment movement appears to have started on the Common for Lord Onslow leased small plots to soldiers returning from the Napoleonic Wars @ 2 shilings p.a. p.a. and moved the Allotment Act of 1831. The leases given by Lord Onslow for brick clay extraction brought him into conflict with the commoners in one of only two cases of litigation against a Lord of the Manor (1870). The outcome was a compromise in which Lord Onslow received 200 acres of the Common and agreed not to issue leases for clay digging. The 200 acres became building land for Sunningdale.
A History of Chobham Common Joy Mason 1994 31pp

Coxes Lock Mill is now flats but survived as a working flour mill until 1983. It had kept up with advances in mill technology having water turbines and roller mills and latterly electric power. Grain arrived by barge from London Docks and there were good road and rail connections. The first mill was built in 1776 to exploit the water supply of the Navigation. From 1783 to 1829 there was an iron forging mill as well as the flour mill and part of the latter was used as a silk mill from 1834. The tall building dates from 1900.

Cowey Stakes is the side of the Thames between Walton Bridge and the Desborough Cut. Stakes are found in the river bed. Here, some claim, Julius Caesar's army crossed the Thames during his second expedition to Britain but the same claim is made elsewhere. The name is said to derive from a ford marked by stakes for drovers taking cattle across.

A **Curfew Bell** rings at Chertsey church at 8pm. Neville Audley found sanctuary in the abbey to avoid decapitation after the Lancastrian defeat in the Battle of Barnet. Yorkists threatened the abbey so, expecting a reprieve, he promised to emerge at curfew. The king's messenger was delayed at the ferry and Neville's lover Blanche Heriot clung to the clapper to stop the curfew bell ringing. This myth comes from a play of 1842 by Albert Smith and was popularised 10 years later by Rose Harwick's poem, *Curfew must not ring tonight*, re-set in the Civil War with the reprieve coming from Cromwell.

Tales of Old Surrey Matthew Alexander Countryside Books 1985 95pp

The **Desborough Cut** was made in 1935 (job creation scheme?) and the land enclosed within the meanders of the river became Desborough Island.

Emmetts Mill on the Mill Bourne is a residence made from the 18th century millhouse where stood a 14th century abbey mill. Emmett was miller in 1577.

Fairoaks Airport was a farmer's private airstrip in the 1930s and became Dolley's Farm flying station in World War II for initial pilot training in Tiger Moths. The RAF retained it until 1966 and the runway was grass until 1978. It is now an aviation business complex with commercial airport for light aircraft.

Surrey Airfields in the Second World War Len Pilkington Countryside Books 1997

The **fishponds** were probably part of the fish farm constructed by Chertsey Abbey when Rutherwyke was Abbott 1307-40. Gracious Pond near the bend in the eponymous lane was filled in around 1870. The splendid Gracious Pond Farmhouse may be on the site of the piscatorial brothers' house. *Gracious* is possibly derived from a person's name for it was Cratchettes pond in 1461.

Goldsworth was a hamlet which gave its name to the most outlying tithing of Woking Parish which also included the hamlets of Brookwood and Knaphill. It was *Goldhord* in a deed of 1229 which suggests the origin of the name.

Gordon's School was founded in 1885 as a memorial to the general killed the same year in Khartoum. Initially it provided artisan training for boys who had left school at 14, to fit them for civilian or military life. Now it is a minor public school with 600 boys and girls. A statue of Gordon on camel is visible from the Chobham road - repatriated by the Sudanese at Independence.

Gordon and the Gordon Boys School Lt Col G S Hutchinson 1944 GBS 56pp

Heath occurs in low rainfall areas on sandy soils deficient in calcium - badland probably caused by forest clearance of Neolithic farmers. Humus will not gel on the sand particles in the absence of calcium so the soil does not hold water, nutrients and microbes. Only a specialized flora can survive.

Horsell Common is open to the public for recreational use but is private land owned by its Preservation Society. Until the start of the 20th century it was regulated and used like other commons but in 1910 the lord of the manor, Lord Onslow, put its management in the hands of a group of residents who became trustees. They bought the freehold in 1960 and registered the society in 1961. About half the 810 acres are an SSSI. Horsell was part of the Pyrford manor from Domesday Book times until 1815. It has an ancient parish church but no "big house". The church has features dated to 1320 but may be older for Newark Abbey was granted the advowson in 1258. The village expanded at the same time as Woking and merged with Woking UDC in 1907.

Lock 15 on the Basingstoke Canal is the first of the steep Deepcut series, climbing 29m/95 feet to Lock 28.

Longcross probably gets its name from a cross used as a boundary marker for Chertsey, Egham and Chobham. It was a hamlet of Chertsey which became a parish in 1847 when the landowner William Tringham built the church to save his neighbours and workers the journey to Chertsey. He was not all good for he also bought the two public houses and extinguished their licenses. It was he who built the first Longcross House. This was replaced by another in 1931 and by the present house in 1994. The church is unusual in lying on a north-south axis. *The story of Longcross* H J F Tringham 1934 24pp

The **London - Southampton** railway line: see box on page 39.

Paragon, built 1998-2003, is the HQ of the TAG-McLaren Group providing space for all company activities, research, factory, training, admin and museum. It replaced 18 buildings mainly in the Woking area. McLarens only develop and build racing cars though sister companies develop and sell electronic equipment for vehicles and leisure.

Mimbridge appears as a boundary mark for Chobham with Chertsey Abbey's 13th century copy of a charter of 673. The name perhaps deriving from *mint*. The bridge crosses the Bourne.

The **Monastery** in Brookwood Cemetery, occupied by the Brotherhood of St Edward the Martyr, occupies the original Anglican chapel of the cemetery and its church was the second Anglican chapel. The adjacent raised areas are the remains of the platform of the cemetery railway terminus. The monastery was created in 1984 as a shrine and chantry for St Edward and to service the church for the Orthodox community. Edward was the Saxon king of all England, 975-979, after the death of his father, Edgar, and was crowned at Kingston. His bones were found at Shaftesbury Abbey by archæologists in 1931 and after theft and legal wrangling were brought here. *The Criminologist* Vol 5, Nos 16/17 May/August 1970 (St Edward's bones)

The **Muslim Cemetery** was started in 1915 to counter German disinformation that sepoys were not receiving proper death rites. The 28 were re-interred in Brookwood cemetery in 1969. (Hindu sepoys were cremated at Brighton).

The **Nauticalia Ferry** normally operates on the half hour but continuously if very busy. Weekdays 8-6; weekends 9-5. This is where the towing path changed sides so the Nauticalia boatmen are of antique lineage.

Newark Mill was a great wooden building with three wheels but burned down in 1966. It was probably on the site of the Send mill listed in the Domesday Book for 21s 6d tax.

Newark Priory was initiated by Ruald de Calric during the reign (1189-99) of Richard the Lionheart. It was a new place for the Augustinian canons. The building is 13th century but overlies an earlier church. It was endowed with gifts of land round about and in London, whose ownership is still remembered in place names with *priory,* eg at Hurtmore and Puttenham. It also held the advowsons of many local churches and provided their vicars eg Windlesham, Send, Horsell, Pyrford, Pirbright, Woking, West Clandon and St Martha's.

Occam's Razor is now a saw of science. William of Occam (1290?-1349) is thought to have originated from Ockham and the village attracts visitors from all over the world because of him. A friar, educated at the Franciscan house in Oxford, he taught at the University of Paris and figures in the development of logic, philosophy and political theory. As an ecclesiastical rebel he was a forerunner of Martin Luther (1483-1546). He led a splinter group of Franciscans demanding evangelical poverty. Having accused Pope John XII of 70 errors and 7 heresies, he was excommunicated in 1330 and placed under house arrest at Avignon. Aided and protected by the Holy Roman Emperor, the Bavarian, Louis IV, he escaped and spent the rest of his life in Munich where he is commemorated by Occamstraße. The razor is: *Entia non sunt multiplicanda præter necessitatem* - entities are not to be multiplied without necessity. In science, if several solutions or explanations are possible, the simplest is best until further evidence contradicts it.

Ockham was a traditional English estate until the demise of the Lovelace Family just after WWII. The land and all the houses belonged to the Lord of the Manor and it was self sufficient with a building and maintenance department, home farm, mill, church and manor house. The Earls of Lovelace were lineal descendants of Peter King, Lord Chancellor (1725), who bought the estate in 1710. The village is small - a few cottages spread along the roads. Tyrell Racing cars were made in Ockham parish until recently. The manor was BOCHEHÃ in the Domesday Book, with a clerical error, B. William the Conqueror gave it to his soldier, Richard FitzGilbert. Ockham Church, All Saints, may have some of the fabric of the Domesday Book church but the greater part of the nave and chancel walls date from around 1220. It is a typical village church having many alterations from later periods. Features of interest: the 7-lancet east window, c1250; the monument to Lord King in the King chapel; the ceilings with all the roof bosses different; the doorway of the rood loft high up beside the chancel arch; the 3-course tower c1500; the west window of the north aisle commemorating the 700th anniversary of the birth of William of Ockham.

Ockham Mill is now a splendid residence with the ornamental brickwork favoured by the Lovelaces of the Ockham estate. The building dates from 1862 but milling stopped in 1927. The wheel is internal, 14' 6" diameter, 9' 10" wide. There has been a mill here since at least 1296.

Watermills of Surrey Derek Stidder 1990 Barracuda Books 1990 144pp

Ockham Park house was built in 1629 for Henry Weston. This Jacobean house was transformed under the direction of Nicholas Hawksmoor into an Italianate mansion in the 1830s. The main house has been rebuilt since the serious fire of 1948 but the stable and orangery are as before.

Ottershaw Park rose in 1908 to replace the Palladian brick house built by Thomas Sewell, Master of the Rolls in the 1760s. Only the twin lodges built to the design by James Wyatt in 1796 survive on the end of Coach Road. Lord Brabazon, later 12th Earl of Meath leased the park in the 1880s which is when the Countess associated herself with the initiation of the Meath Home at Godalming. The garden area is now a housing estate. The house has been Ottershaw College and the Mobiloil HQ but is now divided into apartments.

Papercourt Farm gave its name to the lock and the gravel pit lake. The earliest form is *Pappeworth* in 1204 meaning Pappa's Farm. *Court* appears to have been added as an embellishment.

Pirbright is not a Domesday Book manor but was probably cut from Woking Manor by Henry I for his son Robert, Duke of Gloucester. The last notable Lord of the Manor, Lord Pirbright, lived at Henley Park. Many pre-WWI cottages, bear the estate logo. The village hall on the green was a gift of Lord Pirbright. The church, St Michael and All Angels, is Georgian but there was a church as early as 1200, deduced from a charter witnessed by Jordan, parson of PIREFRICTH (facsimile in church). The grave of **Stanley** the explorer, is in the churchyard.   *The Day before Yesterday - the story of Pirbright* Helen Yool

The **pump** just below Lock 1 was installed in 2001. It sends water back above Lock 6 via a 30cm pipe under or beside the towpath, allowing the locks to be used during water shortage through Woking - the most used part of the canal.

Pyrford has been part of Woking since 1933. Before 19th century building it had two clusters of farmhouses. The one around the old church is little altered; the other has become large housing estates. PYRIANFORD first appears in a charter of King Eadwig granting land to Eadrid in 956. In the Domesday Book it is PELIFORDE. William the Conqueror gave it to Westminster Abbey.

Pyrford Church, St Nicholas, is no longer at the centre of modern Pyrford. It is Norman, one of the oldest churches in Surrey, almost in its original form though with some of the windows altered. Points of interest: fragments of wall paintings of 1200 and 1140, 12th century chancel and door arches, 14th century east window, Tudor pews, pulpit of 1628.

Pyrford Place is now a block of modern apartments but the summerhouse on the canal bank is the original Tudor building. John Donne lived here after being undone by marrying the 17 year old Anne More of Loseley in 1601.

Ripley is, historically, a satellite of Send. High Street was the A3 and the old London to Portsmouth road hence the nautical pub names. *The Talbot* with Georgian façade was the post house and looks much as it would have in stage-coach days. The Green is said to be the largest in England; cricket has been played on it since about 1700, the club dating from 1743. The church, St Mary Magdelene, was rebuilt in 1846 onto the Norman chancel. A round window in the south aisle commemorates Herbert Liddell Cortis the first to cycle 20 miles in an hour. The twin lodges in Newark Lane are 1939 Tudoresque.

St John's village formed around the wharf after the canal came though. The bridge got its name from a brick kiln. The Victorian Gothic church originated as a chapel-of-ease to (Old) Woking parish church in 1840 and provided the name. St John's became a separate parish in 1883.

The **sandpit** in Horsell Common is where *The War of the Worlds* starts (pub. 1898). The narrator sees a flash on Mars, from a friend's observatory in Ottershaw, then a large metal cylinder falls upon the Common. Travellers on the Woking and Chobham roads are attracted to the crater by the mass of spectators and zapped by ray gun. There were evidently few trees when H G Wells (1866-1946) lived in Woking. *War of the Worlds* H G Wells Everyman 1993

The **Semaphore Tower** is open to the public in the afternoons during weekends and Bank Holidays from mid-March to October (☎ 01372 458822). It was restored in 1989 and the signalling mechanism may be operated by visitors. The arms slot into the mast when at rest. The tower is 60½ feet tall and was built in 1822 as part of the chain of semaphore or telegraph stations from the Admiralty to Portsmouth, prompted by the Napoleonic Wars. The adjacent stations were on Cabbage Hill to the NE and Pewley Hill, Guildford to the SW. A branch chain from Chatley Heath to Plymouth was abandoned in 1832, before completion. Its first station was a similar tower beside the church in Worplesdon. The other stations were either bungalows or 3 storey houses.

The Old Telegraphs Geoffrey Wilson 1976 Phillimore 252pp

Send is a network of ribbon development along the roads but in Saxon times would have been a mile away near the church and river. It was the Domesday Book SANDE, a manor taxed for 20 hides, two mills and five fisheries.

Send Church, St Mary the Virgin, has a chancel dating from about 1240 with the original lancet windows on the south side. The nave was rebuilt in the 14th century and the timber porch added late in the 15th. A church is listed for Send in the Domesday Book, presumably on this site.

Send Pound has been restored as the small fenced area next to a garden. From medieval times it was where stray cattle were impounded. A peasant farmer usually had only one milking cow and one or two plough oxen - not the herd of a present-day farmer.

Shepperton appears as SCEPERTONE in SPELETORNE Hundred on the Middlesex folios of the Domesday Book. Westminster Abbey was Lord of the Manor but operated it as a normal manor with 17 villeins and a priest. The church, St Nicholas, on the river bank in the old village, was built in 1614 and had the oblong tower added around 1700. Next to it, the rectory is a 7-bay timber framed hall of about 1500 concealed by later wings and mathematical tiles. The 12th century church is known from a drawing and appears to have suffered from floods; medieval wills included money to pay for piles for it.

Shepperton Lock was constructed in an artificial cut in 1813. A weir had been taxed for 6s 8d in the Domesday Book presumably for its flash lock revenue. In 1293 the Bishop of London was taking tolls for a dam and sluice.

Stanley (1841-1904) of "Dr Livingstone, I presume" fame retired to Furze Hill in the parish of Pirbright. Illegitimate, he grew up in a Welsh workhouse, fought in the American civil war and became a *New York Herald* journalist. His great *coup* was the expedition to central Africa to find Livingstone who had been "lost" trying to establish that Lake Tanganyika was the source of the Nile; they met at Ujiji, November 1871. In a second expedition he continued Livingstone's work, following the Lualaba River down to the sea to find it was the Congo, not the Nile. When employed by the Belgian king to set up a chain of trading stations Stanley became the creator of the Congo (now Zaire) and a catalyst for the carve up of Africa by the European powers. Wielding a sledge-hammer brought him the African name *Bula Mutari* - smasher of rocks.

Stanley - Making of an African Explorer (Biography Vol 1) Frank McLynn Constable 1989 411pp
Stanley - Sorcerer's Apprentice (Biography Vol 2) Frank McLynn Constable 1991 499pp

Tank Factory is local vernacular for the military vehicle research station which changed its official name frequently. It started in 1942 when the government requisitioned part of Chobham Common for testing tanks and went on to develop technology and testing for all sorts of fighting land vehicles. The test track is now leased for road testing of civilian vehicles. Chobham Armour was devised here.

Tank Hill, like the other hills near the M3 is capped by ice-age plateau gravels. Permission to fly model aircraft appears in the 1935 minutes of Chobham Common and the knolls at the west end of the hill are the spiritual home of several clubs. To the south the North Downs can be seen with the notch where the River Wey cuts through at Guildford.

Thames Lock, at the outlet of the Wey Navigation, is manned because it is the toll collecting point and because the 3rd gate sometimes has to be used. This was added in the 1820s when the Navigation was extended downstream to reach deeper water after Shepperton Lock lowered the Thames.

Thorpe widely known for the theme park was one of the earliest places to be documented in England. It was Torpe in the 673 charter, as part of the gift of land to Chersey Abbey, and TORP four centuries later in the Domesday Book. Þorp (Thorp) was a Saxon word for village. The church, St Mary's, has 12th century work but is much restored. The American School, TASIS, is there.

Trigg's Lock on the Wey Navigation is at a point where the river and canal re-join. The lock-keeper's main function is to regulate the water levels with the sluices. Formerly he would have collected tolls. The house bears a fire mark.

The **vineyards** at Send are operated by Valley Vineyards, Twyford, on buffer land of the gravel extraction company. Pinot Noire, Gamay, Müller Türgau & Seyval Blanc are grown. In a superlative year the 5 acres can produce 12 tons to make 12,000 bottles. Bernard Theobald pioneered the planting here.

Walsham Gates on the Wey Navigation are sited where the canal and river separate and are used as a lock only at flood times to stop too much water entering the canal. The turf sided lock is primitive - not lined with masonry. The lock keepers' main job is adjusting the sluice gates to maintain the water level for upstream navigation; originally he would also have collected tolls.

Walton-on-Thames was the Domesday Book manor of WALETONE. A timber -framed gable of the Tudor manor house can be seen from the river. John Bradshaw, who pronounced sentence on Charles I, lived there. The first bridge opened in 1750 of timber braced arches; it is known from a painting of Canaletto. The later bridge of stone and brick opened in 1780. Turner painted this bridge by moonlight. Pevsner comments only a contractor would be prepared to paint the iron third bridge of 1864. At the time of writing a new bridge is expected to replace temporary iron girder road bridge of 2000. The Bailey bridge beside it for pedestrians was the WWII replacement for the Victorian iron bridge. The crossing was freed of tolls for £7000 in 1870. To be rowed to Walton Bridge from London Bridge cost 1s 9d in 1820.

West End expanded in the 19th century from a hamlet in the adminstrative west half of Chobham Parish. Gordon's School is there. It had its own church, Holy Trinity from 1890 and became an ecclesiastical parish in 1895.

The River **Wey** has two main tributaries, each called Wey, the northern one rising at Alton and the southern from many springs near Haslemere and Selborne . The confluence is at Tilford. The main river runs from there via Godalming to Guildford, where the Cranleigh Water and Tilling Bourne join it, then skirts passes Old Woking on its way to join the Thames at Weybridge.

The **Wey Navigation** from Weybridge to Guildford was made by improving the river bed and making cuts - the first artificial waterway of any length in Britain. Caen stone in the arches of Pyrford church (Norman) suggests the river was already in use for transport. The Navigation was approved by Act of Parliament in 1651 but the instigator, Sir Richard West of Sutton Place, had already made a cut across a loop of the river in his grounds and built a lock at Stoke (juxta Guildford) around 1620, further development being delayed by the Civil War. The 15½ route miles are 9 miles of canal segments between stretches of the river with 12 locks. The last private owner, Harry Stevens, gave the Navigation to the National Trust in 1964 but commercial use persisted between Tilbury Docks and Coxes (flour) Mill until 1983. Unlike the Basingstoke Canal it is never short of water and the locks may be freely used; so narrow boats are to be seen on the move all the year round.
London's Lost Route to the Sea P A L Vine David & Charles 1973 267pp

Weybridge was WAIGEBRUGG in the Saxon charter of 675 endowing Chersey Abbey, presumably taking its name from a predecessor of the present iron bridge. In the Domesday Book it was WEBRUGE in the Elmbridge Hundred. and is now in Elmbridge Borough. In 1463 Thomas Warner was granted a license for a wharf at the mouth of the Wey.

Wisley is the vernacular name for the Royal Horticultural Society's garden but is an ancient village on the banks of the River Wey to the north of the garden, WISELEI in the Domesday Book. When the sewage works were being built near the church, signs of neolithic and Iron Age villages were found with a quernstone and 5 pottery kilns.

Wisley Airfield opened with a grass runway during WWII to test aircraft from the nearby Brooklands factory of Vickers, including the Wellington bomber. Its potential is said to have been spotted by a test pilot, "Mutt" Summers, who crash landed on the farmland in the 1930s. It was used for prototype flight trials, engine testing, kitting out and storage of aircraft awaiting distribution and had workshops and test sheds. The concrete runway was laid in 1952 and saw the proving flights of the Viking, Viscount, Valiant, Vanguard, BAC-111 and VC10. Heathrow's development and proximity was one of the reasons for the British Aircraft Corporation closing it in 1973.
Surrey Airfields in the Second World War Len Pilkington Countryside Books 1997

Wisley Church was built around 1140 and retains its original form though some windows and the roof have been replaced. Points of interest: chalk chancel arch, Norman windows, gothic windows of 1627, the Black Prince in the list of patrons, Elizabethan hour glass bracket over pulpit, the sarsen by the door which probably caused the church to be sited here.

The **Wisley Garden** of the Royal Horticultural Society is open every day except Christmas. The inaugural meeting of the society was in 1804 after an initial suggestion from John Wedgewood (son of Josiah) to William Forsyth, George III's gardener. The garden started as 1½ acres in South Kensington. but in 1823 moved to a 33 acre site in Chiswick and was soon actively searching in China and North America for new plants to bring to Britain. The royal charter was awarded in 1861. The Wisley site was a 60 acre private garden started in 1878. Sir Thomas Hanbury bought it as a gift for the RHS in 1903 "for the purpose of an Experimental Garden and the Encourage-ment and Improvement of Scientific and Practical Horticulture in all its branches". The society has added more land so the garden is now 240 acres.

Wisley - The Royal Horticultural Society's Garden M&A Rix 1989 Julian Holland

Woking first appears in writing as *Wocchingas* around 710 when the village, Old Woking, was on the river. New Woking mushroomed in the 19th century. The canal was operating by 1796 and the railway by 1838 but did not cause growth because the land was Common which could not be sold. An Act of Parliament in 1852 enabled the Necropolis Company to buy 2600 acres of Woking Common for the (Brookwood) cemetery, most of which was sold for building. Small parcels were sold to numerous builders, houses rose higgledy piggledy on the heath tracks and there was no urban authority, hence the chaotic roads. Woking did not become an Urban District Council until 1895. Modern councils have struggled to give Woking a centre and through ways.

A History of Woking Allan Crosby 1982 Phillimore 224pp

Old Woking was the village of WOCHINGES manor in the Domesday Book, a large royal estate with church and mill. Granted away by King John, it reverted to the crown through inheritance. The manor house became a royal palace. The church, St Peter, was founded around 675, according to a papal letter of 710, the earliest reference to Woking. It was an outpost of the monks of Medeshamstead, now called Peterborough. The oldest parts of the present church are the Norman west and north walls of the nave. The Norman door-way now opens into the base of the tower which was added around 1200 and the door itself is thought to be the original one of around 1080. Points of interest: replacement windows of the nave, 1350 next to the Zouche gallery; east window around 1350; mid-15th century oak pews; 15th & 17th century chests; Purdan brass 1523; Shadan brass 1527.

Woking Mill is probably on the site of the Domesday Book mill. Until 1835 it supplied flour for London made from wheat bought at the Guildford market then it became a paper mill which had 136 workers in 1870. Unwin Brothers bought it when they were displaced by fire from their mill at Chilworth in 1896 and added the Dutch gables. Three turbines drove the machinery and water still spews from three conduits under the building.

Woking Palace was a favoured home of Henry VIII, many letters being signed there. It is said Wolsey heard of his elevation to cardinal when visiting. The palace has now gone but the moat is still visible and a grey outbuilding still stands (visible from the Navigation). It was set in a deer park, three miles in circumference, stretching northwards. Edward VI and Queen Elizabeth used it but in 1620 James I granted the manor to Edward Zouche who took the stone for his new house, Hoe Bridge Place, in the village.

The Ruins of old Woking Palace D J Haggard Surrey Archæological Collections vol 55 1958